Arthur Eaton lives in the beautiful city of Cambridge in East Anglia. After working in the Space Industry, his engineering career brought him to 'Silicon Fen', a hot bed for technological and biological research. But it's also a city that breathes history with its most famous university founded in the medieval age by Henry II in 1209. This has rekindled Arthur's childhood passion for history, redirecting his engineering and science trained mind to delve deep into the past.

MEDIEVAL EUROPEAN EMPIRES COPY

EARLY NATIONS OF FIFTH-CENTURY EUROPE TO THE RENAISSANCE

ARTHUR EATON

INDEPENDENTLY PUBLISHED

...

ISBN 978-1-915651-00-6 PB

ISBN 978-1-915651-01-3 HB

...

Cover Image: The Death of Olaf II at the Battle of Stiklestad by Peter Nicolai Arbo (1831 - 1892)

To Rose-Anna

My constant and loving companion who knows I am
happiest when presented with a good meal

CONTENTS

MAPS

Europe in the Medieval Age

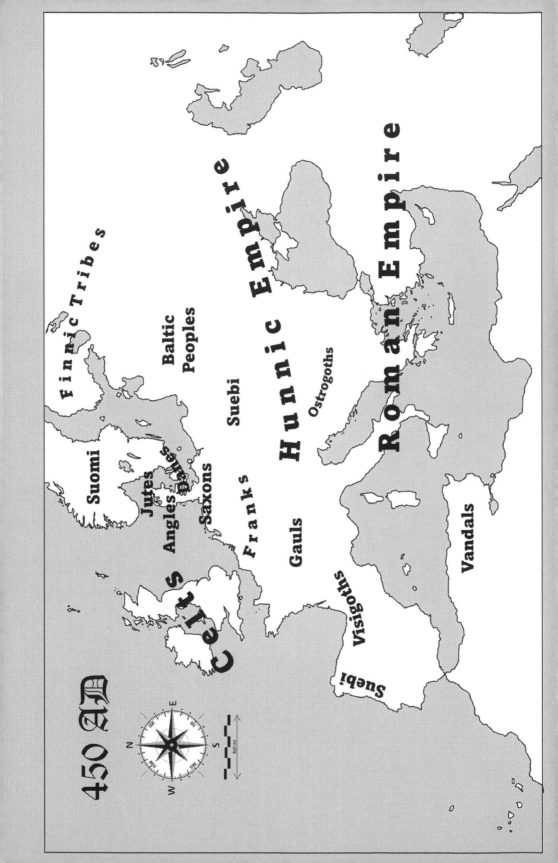

450 AD

Finnic Tribes

Suomi

Baltic Peoples

Suebi

Jutes
Angles
Danes
Saxons

Celts

Franks

Gauls

Hunnic Empire

Ostrogoths

Roman Empire

Visigoths

Suebi

Vandals

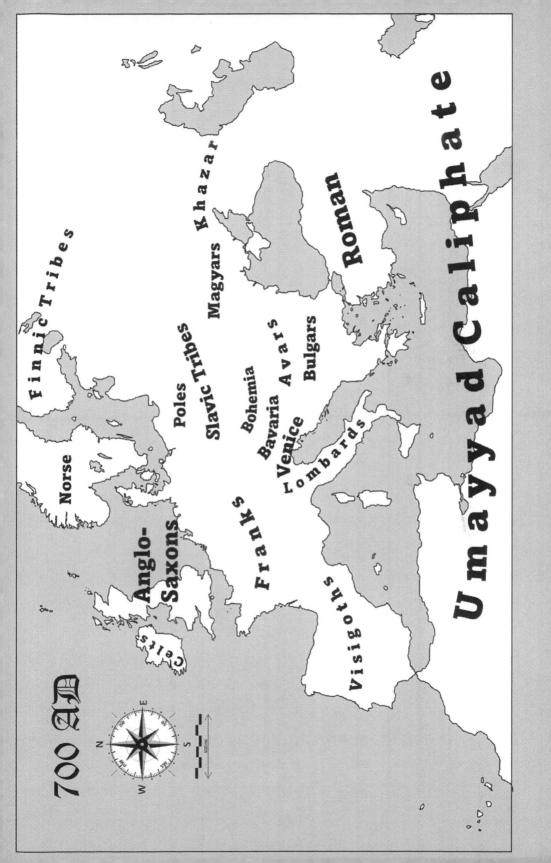

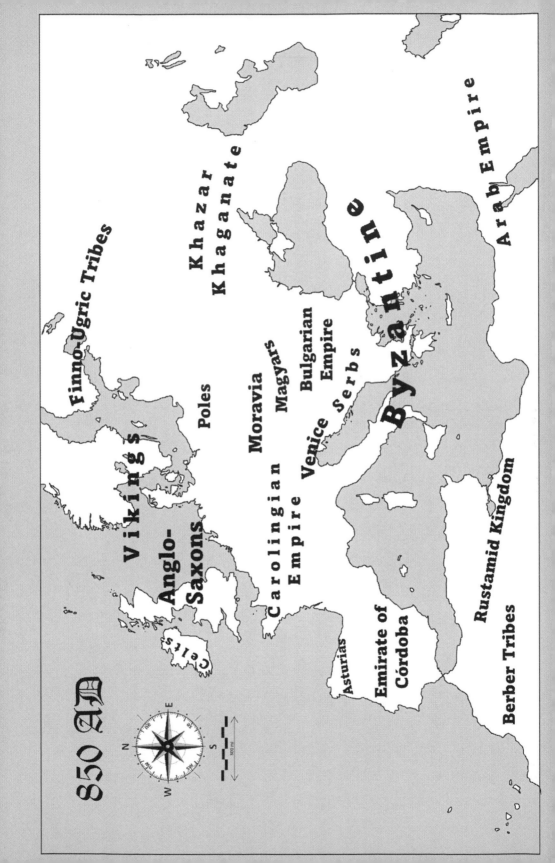

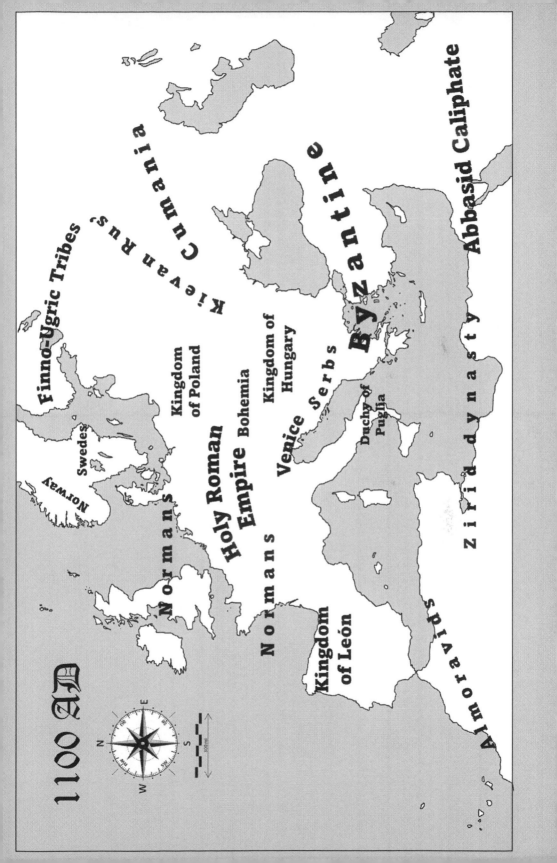

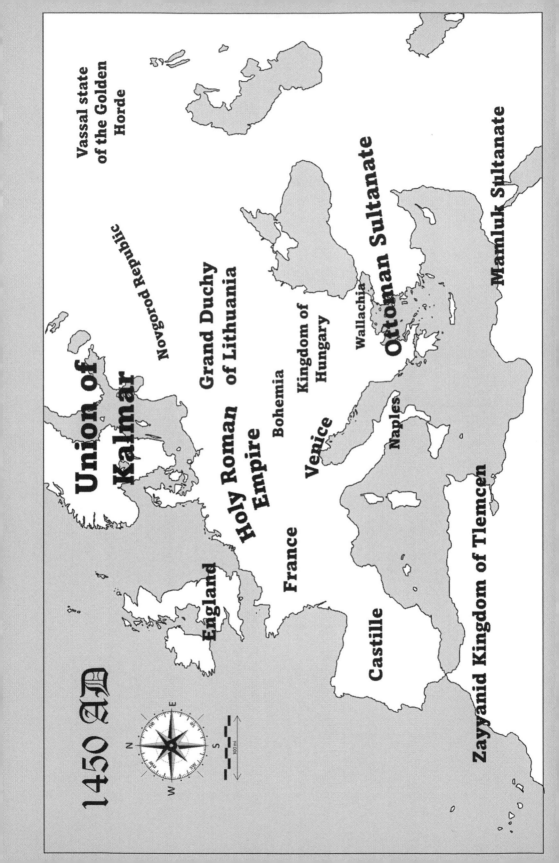

INTRODUCTION

Civilization is a movement and not a condition, a voyage and not a harbor.

–Arnold J. Toynbee

There is much knowledge inherent in language. Anglo-Saxon and Indo-European surnames like the typically British 'Smith,' 'Fisher,' or 'Shepherd,' commonplace German surnames 'Fischer,' 'Schneider,' or 'Weber,' or French surnames 'Boucher,' 'Chevrolet,' 'Granger,' or 'Fournier' were not the result of some creative whim. Rather, they were inspired by the trade of our ancestors. If you come from an Anglo-Saxon or Indo-European tradition, you can learn something about your ancestors from looking at your surname.

The English 'Smith,' the German 'Schmidt,' and the Italian 'Ferrari' (1) reveal that your ancestors were mostly smiths—using heat, they melted metal to create tools and weapons—while Fisher or Fischer meant your lineage derives from a group of historical fishermen. 'Weber' is German for 'weaver,' someone who weaved textiles, while 'Schneider' translates to 'tailor.' If you come from an Anglo-Saxon heritage (2), you will discover the occupations of your ancestors simply by looking at your surname. The same applies to other Indo-European nations such as the French. 'Boucher' translates to 'butcher,' 'Fournier' means 'baker,' 'Granger' speaks about "a type of farm worker" while the most famous on the list, 'Chevrolet,' was none other than a goat herder.

As mentioned above, there is much knowledge that can be uncovered simply from studying language. After the Western Roman Empire collapsed, a number of other nations and empires emerged and, as a consequence, there were the births of Anglo-Saxon and Indo-European nations. Looking at these surnames, what we learn is not that Europe fell into darkness once the light closed on the Western Roman Empire, but rather that industry and commerce continued, if not flourished, in Europe.

While labor is typically menial, it is and was—more so historically—the foundation of commerce, trade, and development in Europe. You might be disappointed—if your lineage comes from an Indo-European or Anglo-Saxon tradition—to find that your family were simply commoners or laborers, but it was the fruits of their labor in which some of the greatest empires were born.

While it is true that the Mediterranean trade route was especially active during the Bronze and Classical Ages, it continued to act in such a manner in the Middle Ages. Trade did not stop via the Mediterranean channel; it just became somewhat delayed as it was often directed to the Muslim world, Byzantium (3), or Asia, and afterwards commodities and resources were shared with Europe.

It is true that when the Roman Empire collapsed, Catholicism became a dominant force in Europe. That being said, the whole continent did not convert immediately to this religion. First, conversion to Catholicism occurred at a slow pace. In fact, it was only until the later Middle Ages—almost coinciding with the Renaissance—that many groups of people converted. Second, for much of the period, the majority of populations did not adhere to Christian beliefs. A lot of pagan rituals and customs continued to be practiced. And in some cases, pagan rites were also adopted by some Christian denominations. While there were groups of individuals converting to this religion, many of them continued to practice their pagan rituals and customs.

As we will see in the first chapter, historians from the Renaissance—following the Middle Ages—viewed the spread of Christianity through Europe inspiring the period to be called the Dark Ages. Yet, religious belief was not something the masses subscribed to and the spread of Catholicism was delayed. The historians and thinkers believed that it was the religious institutionalism which delayed the advance of many subjects such as astronomy, mathematics, medicine, and the pursuit of knowledge. However, many Christian monks and adherents encouraged literary and artistic avenues while also promoting engagement with sciences such as medicine and astronomy. One thing you should keep in mind is that there were also archaic and pagan beliefs which held people back like human and animal sacrifice, which became outlawed under Constantine's son Constantius II in 341 CE. Naturally, Catholicism and other variations of Christian doctrine still maintained some outdated beliefs—certainly outdated by today's standards—but there were many implemented by these religious institutions which did a lot of good, like the outlawing of sacrifice. Even surely, the Renaissance thinkers looking at the so-called "Dark Ages" would have to admit that these times were less dark because fewer humans and animals were sacrificed.

Fascination with history started when I was a child. I imagined people learning to survive without modern conveniences such as electricity, cars, televisions and a thousand other such things. Yet survive they did, developing their cultures as I wrongly thought - in isolation. Picking up my first history book, I soon realized my mistake. Contact between different peoples, trade and war existed all the way back into prehistoric times. That realization made the past all that more intriguing and enchanting.

As said, there is a misconception that the light of civilization went out in Europe when the Roman Empire disintegrated, but one of my favorite periods to study was the "Dark Ages." That is one of the main reasons which brought me to writing this book.

First, I simply am infatuated with Medieval Europe. Naturally, anything historical fascinates me, whether it is the Persian or Mongolian empires or the Qin Shin Huang Dynasty, but there is something special about Medieval Europe. Perhaps it is because Europe has never been conquered by one nation. Second, I wanted to dispel the belief that Medieval Europe was simply a continent lost in darkness. Surely, the breakthroughs and incredible achievements of the Renaissance could not have come out of thin air. Scientific, astronomical, and philosophical discoveries of the Renaissance and later the Age of Enlightenment must have been based on some foundation created in Medieval Europe. Lastly, the Medieval Period saw a number of advanced empires, some enduring longer than we think, like the Holy Roman Empire.

Medieval Roman Empires will relate some of the most exciting European empires. While it aims to follow a chronological order—beginning with the Hunnic Empire who have been attributed as one of the causes of the Roman Empire's dissolution to the Kalmar Union which survived to see the early Renaissance—there is overlap with many of the empires. In each section, we will cover the aspects of each empire: geographical location, origins of the empire, key figures and leaders, significant events and battles, the principal customs and culture, interesting facts, and finally, what brought about its downfall. For example, the Holy Roman Empire emerged in the 10th century but only saw its dissolution in the 19th century, with later entries such as the Kalmar Empire and the Grand Duchy of Lithuania.

CHAPTER ONE

THE MEDIEVAL PERIOD:

MORE THAN JUST A PLACEHOLDER

B old as it may be to say, one of the greatest setbacks in history is that the Dark Ages (Middle Ages or Medieval Period) will simply forever be known as the Dark Ages. The word 'dark' was a term coined by the historian Petrarch. It implies that Europe entered an intellectual 'darkness' after the Roman Empire collapsed and that all progress in the continent seemingly halted. More recently, it has become referred to as the Middle Ages or Medieval Period.

Even 'Middle' or 'Medieval'—literally meaning Middle Ages from the Latin *medium aevum*—hardly suggests anything noteworthy taking place from 500 to about 1200 CE. Prior ages such as the Stone Age, Iron Age, or Bronze Age, as basic as they are, imply technological advancement. The Stone Age reveals that we mastered stone tools, while the Bronze and Iron Ages indicate that we wielded these metals to craft more advanced tools. Names of periods such as the Ancient and Classical periods imply a movement to ancient architecture, like the creation of Parthenon, Greek temples and hippodromes, and the pyramids, while the Classical Era evokes imagery of Roman columns and arenas. All connote that a shift took place—each age improving on the strides made by the previous one. Later, the Renaissance, literally meaning "rebirth after the so-called terribly dark Middle Ages" and later the age of Enlightenment, furthered the notion that much knowledge and intellectual progress were attained.

When it comes to the Dark Ages, it simply implies that the Roman Empire collapsed and the light of civilization was lost for 700 years. Europe was swept up into a storm of raiding barbarians and unending violence while the hand of Catholicism stifled progress.

Some of it is true, but that is only half of the story. It is true that the Roman Empire fell, but only the Western half collapsed. The Eastern half, Byzantium, with its capital at Constantinople (today Istanbul [1]) still remained a beacon of light for another 1000 years. In this chapter, we will discuss why the terms "Dark Ages," "Middle Ages," and 'Medieval,' despite having stood the test of time, are insufficient in describing what was 700 years of great progress and development and which saw some of the greatest European empires (2). We will analyze the reasons why the Middle Ages were not simply a placeholder period between the Roman Empire and Renaissance.

The Dark Ages – Misconceptions, Myths, & Facts

Renaissance Thinkers and Historians

The first reason why the term "Dark Ages" was used was owing to a number of historians who held a definitive bias for Greco-Roman culture. There were numerous achievements in Greek and Roman civilizations in terms of architecture, infrastructure such as the creation of aqueducts, and education and literacy. The objective of this book is not to understate the value of these Greco-Roman accomplishments. The problem is that many Renaissance historians tended to overstate these achievements while understating the progress made by empires during the Middle Ages—hence, giving rise to the term Dark Ages. Even before the Renaissance, there were historians who wrote that when the Roman Empire (Western half) had disintegrated, Europe was delivered to the ruthless, untutored Germanic barbarians and evolution stood still. These include St. Jerome and St. Patrick writing in the 5th century, Gregory of Tours a century later, and Bede in the 8th century. These three historians, however, held a Roman-centric bias. In truth, if any civilization had come after and were very much unlike the Greek and Roman Empires, these historians would have most likely believed it to be backward.

During the Renaissance, the Middle Ages truly earned the terrible reputation of being dark, violent, and backward. There were two chief historians who were principally responsible for tarnishing its good name. The first is Edward Gibbon. This historian, Gibbon, is most well-known for his six volumes of *The History of the Decline and Fall of the Roman Empire* which cover the fall of the Roman Empire. Gibbon, like his predecessors, believed that once the Roman Empire disintegrated, Europe was lost to darkness and barbarians. One of his most famous remarks was that the Empire collapsed owing to "the triumph of barbarism [i.e., lack of culture] and religion" (Gibbon, E., 1777).

The other historian we have already encountered. Petrarch held similar views to Gibbon. However, unlike Gibbon, Petrarch was not so much as interested in what caused the Roman Empire to dissolve, but he was part of a growing movement who wished to revive Classical Antiquity. This movement came to be known as Renaissance Humanism.

Renaissance Humanism

Some of the main goals of Renaissance Humanism was to return to Classical Antiquity, thus reviving studies of the Greek and Roman Empires. Historians and academics of this period made it their goal to search for lost Roman and Greek texts. Remember, the Renaissance translates to 'rebirth,' referring to a rebirth of Classical cultures.

It is also interesting that they used the term 'humanism.' At the time, the Christians were considered the only humanists. Using the concept of 'humanism' in Renaissance humanism implied a movement away from Christianity. Remember, Gibbon attributed the fall of the Roman Empire to religion, namely Christianity. Prior to this monotheistic religion, Greek and Roman society was largely pagan, but there was some belief in deities, hence their religions were polytheistic. Therefore, the revival of Greek and Roman thinking during the Renaissance sought to return to Greco-Roman thinking, which meant distancing themselves from Christianity. In this sense, Renaissance humanists like Petrarch believed that studying the Classical texts such as the Greek tragedies and epic poems were one such way that this humanism could be achieved.

One of the most poignant examples of this return to the Classical Civilizations is captured in the art of the Renaissance. For those of you who are art lovers, you remember how themes of Classical Civilizations were typical themes of Renaissance painters such as Sandro Botticelli and Raphael. It is Raphael's *The School of Athens* which highlights the praise for Classical culture more so than others. In his painting, the Mathematician Pythagoras, the philosophers Plato and Aristotle, and the mathematician and astronomer Ptolemy are present. So are Archimedes and Euclid, from which Euclidean geometry was born. In Raphael's fresco, there is a gathering of these Greek heroes—a reminder to sixteenth-century Italy of brilliant thinkers that once walked the earth.

While it was true that there was much to be gained from studying the Classical manuscripts and cultures of the Classical period, there was an overemphasis on it. Historians like Petrarch overlooked the significance of the Middle Ages. It is true that literacy among the European population declined somewhat during these 700 years, but once again that is only half the story. Still, the damage was done. Due to Renaissance humanist thinkers such as Petrarch and historians such as Gibbon, the Dark Ages continue to be known as the Dark Ages or the placeholder name, Middle Ages.

MEDIEVAL ACADEMIC EXCELLENCE

One of the principal reasons that the term 'Dark' was used was because there was the belief that Europe entered a time where there was little pursuit of academic excellence. In other words, the 'darkness' that Europe experienced was a darkness of intellectual capacity, a so-called "night of reason" as historian David Bentley Hart puts it. It was also seemingly a darkness experienced by the arts and literature. In Renaissance thinking, the aptitude and necessity of artistic expression too simply was put out. However, there is much evidence that contradicts Renaissance perspectives. First, the oldest university in Europe—and the world—which currently exists is the University of Bologna. It was built in 1088 in Italy's Emilia-Romagna region. Following it are the University of Oxford opened in 1167, with construction starting in 1096, and the University of Salamanca established in 1134. In fact, there is a trend of universities being created in Europe during the 11th, 12th, and 13th centuries—just before the dawn of the Renaissance. If Europe had truly undergone a deprivation of academic pursuits, building universities in every country would hardly be the way of bringing about that deprivation.

PRE-INDUSTRIAL BOOM

In the introduction, we already discussed in detail the boom in industry and commerce during the Middle Ages. There was another major expansion during this period—namely, the agricultural boom. While the exact origins of agriculture are judged to be in the Near East, India, China, and other isolated places, agriculture entered Europe at a later stage. During the Middle Ages, not only did agriculture flourish but a number of inventions brought about much prosperity. These include the introduction of the heavy plow, the horse collar, and metal horseshoes. In the case of the heavy plow, it replaced the scratch plow allowing larger volumes of soil to be tilled, mixing deeper pockets of fertile clay soil with the top layer. Horse collars were instrumental in helping horses carry heavier loads. Sarah Pruitt explains, "Another key innovation of the period was the horse collar, which was placed around a horse's neck and shoulders to distribute weight and protect the animal when pulling a wagon or plough" (Pruitt, S., 2016). With metal horseshoes, the industry of laborers such as smiths inspired development not only to agriculture but transportation. First, the metal horseshoes meant horses could carry heavier loads—replacing oxen on farms—but they could also travel further distances, while bearing carriages and carts used in medieval transportation.

As you can see, many of the inventions such as the horse collar and metal shoes were connected with the advances in industry. However, agricultural development took place within the methods and strategies employed. For example, while crop rotation occurred in more primordial periods like during 6000 BC, in the Middle Ages the use of the two-field and three-field systems were used. For much of the early Medieval period, the two-field system was employed—meaning that for one year specific crops would be cultivated on one field, while the second field is left fallow, meaning no sowing of any seeds takes place. This allowed the land to replenish the lost nutrients from the growing of certain crops. If you continuously plant the same crops, that specific pocket of soil will lose essential nutrients, become weak, and eventually erode.

Towards the end of the Middle Ages, the two-field system was replaced with the three-field system, which was a more advanced form of cultivation, giving rise to the concept of crop rotation. Sections of land were divided into three. In the first section, grains such as wheat and rye were sown in the winter, and oats and barley in spring. On the second piece of land, legumes, which are rich in nitrogen, were cultivated. The production of nitrogen-rich legumes in the farms was not only beneficial to the soil, but increased the general nutrition of the population. The three-field system—a more rudimentary form of crop rotation—facilitated overall increased cultivation, greater nutritional levels among the European population, and protected the land so that it can be used in the next few years. It is hard for you or I to appreciate the impact of these agricultural developments, but starvation historically has always been one of humanity's greatest threats. It is only in the last two centuries that humans have managed to get the upper hand of this nemesis.

MEDIEVAL ARTISTRY

One of the accusations Renaissance thinkers made about the Middle Ages is that the arts had flourished during Greco-Roman times but withered during the Middle Ages. It is true that the Greeks and Romans added immensely to the areas of sculpture, epic poems, tragedies, and architecture. However, the field of arts developed immensely during this time, especially the Carolingian Period. They just took on a new form. For example, stain glass, tapestries, and mosaics became especially common. Perhaps owing to their Catholic connotations, both Renaissance and Enlightened thinkers were reluctant to consider some forms artistic. Interestingly, the relief and fresco art pieces enjoyed a much higher rate of survival than their Greco-Roman counterparts. It was also the development of steelwork in this period that allowed for intricate designs on steelwork, which also fared better over many centuries.

Though universities were being built in the later Middle Ages, 15th century thinkers such as Petrarch used the term 'dark' to define this era. Such views lasted until the 19th century. Only in the 20th century did historians scrutinize this perspective. By the mid-20th century, most historians had agreed that these times were never "Dark Ages" at all. Sadly, even though using the term "Dark Ages" had become frowned upon for being inaccurate, it has persisted. The main reason for the term's survival is the countless historical records which describe the Middle Ages as the "Dark Ages." Khan Academy offers more insight.

> Yet, the term has not disappeared. English Heritage is an organization the British government established in the 1980s to manage historic properties in the UK. In 2016 they published a history of Tintagel Castle, an English ruin from the Middle Ages. In their history, the authors repeatedly referenced the "Dark Ages of Britain." (O'Connor, B.B., n.d.)

It is clear that there were many myths about the Dark Ages. Most of them formed from Renaissance thinkers who had a tendency to elevate the Greek and Roman Empires and consider everything in their shadow as lesser. What is more is not only Gibbon and Petrarch's overly elevated opinion of these empires, but their dislike for Christianity—especially Catholicism—that further added to their opinions that Europe had declined in the Middle Ages.

Chronological Breakdown of the Middle Ages

The beginning of the Middle Ages coincides with the fall of the Western Roman Empire. In fact, a single event has been pinpointed as the exact beginning—namely, the sack of Rome.

In 410, Alaric the Visigoth and king of the Visigoths attacked Rome, after negotiations with the current emperor, Honorius, failed. While the invasion only lasted three days, the consequences were severe. Rome's population severely declined. Over the next 10 years, the population decreased from 800,000 civilians to 500,000. Beyond simply the consequence of the sacking, there were two other reasons for this decline.

Many civilians sought refuge and fled the city. Next, Alaric and the Visigoths had invaded Rome to make use of their food supplies. Another factor occurred years before the Gothic pillaging of Rome. The Roman Empire had been divided into two, weakening both halves. The capital of the Western Roman Empire was Rome and the capital of the Eastern Roman Empire was Constantinople. Since the Western Empire's capital had been ravaged, it was clear that the Roman Empire was on the decline.

It is unclear from where the Goths originated. The historian, Jordanes—who we will encounter more in the next chapter—suggests that they came from Scandinavia originally, while others judge them to be from near the Black Sea. What is known is that they were a nomadic Germanic people. Alaric was the king of the Visigoths—one of the main branches of the Goths. The Visigoths were the "Western Goths" and the other branch was the Ostrogoths, or the "Eastern Goths." The Goths were primarily nomadic, and this explains why when the Visigoths sacked Rome—they went for their food supplies.

THE FALL OF THE WESTERN ROMAN EMPIRE

Rome did not fall in a day. Steady disintegration of the Empire occurred in the Western half during the 4th and 5th centuries. The true date when the Empire ended is posited as 4 September 476 CE, after the Germanic Odoacer killed the emperor Romulus Augustulus, who was just a child then. Though the Germanic King crowned himself the new emperor, it was clear that what he was reigning over was just a shadow of what the empire had once been.

While there is much debate as to which empire was or has been the greatest, the Roman Empire is certainly one of the greatest. Not only were the legions superb, but they had expanded in various fields. They inherited Hellenistic culture from the Greeks; the more their frontier extended, the more influential Hellenistic culture became. Naturally, they conquered numerous groups in places such as Britannia (now England and Wales), Gaul (modern-day France), and parts of North Africa; individuals from these conquered groups sought to join the Romans and embraced their culture. Not only did they make incredible strides in architecture, plumbing and channeling water to cities with their aqueducts, and in scientific studies, but they influenced much of modern-day culture.

Thanks to Roman political developments of the time, many countries have borrowed from their creation of democracy. Furthermore, the legal system of countries also has a foundation in Roman law, created more than 2000 years ago. If we think about widely spoken languages such as French and Spanish, both of these are Romance languages, meaning they were based to some degree on Latin. English, the current lingua franca, takes some of its vocabulary from Latin. Medical terms, scientific names, and legal jargon all use Latin, showing the global influence and range this language still has.

Unfortunately, the Roman Empire became a victim of its own success. Historians for the last thousand years have been studying what caused the Roman Empire to disintegrate. As you might expect, there is some contention as to what truly brought about its fall. It is true that there were constant raids and attacks on the Empire by various barbarian or nomadic groups such as the Goths, Huns, Angles, and Saxons, slowly causing the empire to weaken.

However, when I say that the Roman Empire had become a victim of its own success, this is because the Empire had grown so much, meaning that its frontier too had grown—the bigger the empire, the bigger the frontier to defend. Owing to its massive frontier, the legions had become overstretched, incapable of protecting every border, making it vulnerable to raids on multiple frontiers. This book does not aim to cover the subject of the fall of the Roman Empire in great detail, but one thing it wants to highlight is that the Roman Empire was strong and contributed in numerous and unprecedented ways to the world we know now.

Rome was not built in a day. In fact, it took 1,010,450 days to build the empire. It took some hundred years to disintegrate. In some sense, it is understandable why historians such as Bede, Gibbon, and Petrarch believed Europe had been thrown into darkness when this great empire fell; there was much reason to mourn.

From the first to fifth century CE, a number of Germanic peoples moved from parts of southern Scandinavia into southern Europe and Eurasia. It is this mass exodus of Germanic peoples such as the Vandals, Goths, Angles, and Saxons which gave rise to this period being called the Migration Period. As we saw in the section above, it was the sack of Rome by Alaric the Visigoth that was the defining moment of the Western Roman Empire's fall. However, this mass migration occurred earlier, slowly weakening the Empire, for the Romans had to defend themselves from continuous invasions from these peoples.

The dates of the migration period are not precisely known. This movement of peoples in Europe could have ended in 568 CE or later in the 9th century. Generally, the first part of the Medieval Period is believed to have coincided with this event. It seems likely this Period ended in the 9th century as there were two waves of migration. First, it was the Germanic bands mentioned above like the Goths and Angles. Second, bands coming from all parts of the globe such as the Moors into Southern Europe, the Mongols into Eastern Europe, and the Vikings settled throughout the continent.

In some sense, the historians like Petrarch and Gibbon's belief that Europe had entered an area of darkness arose during the Migration Period. First, the Roman Empire extended throughout Western Europe. The emperor, based in the capital of Rome, was a unifying leader. Later, during the Early Middle Ages, this central leadership was lost when the Western Empire collapsed. The Catholic Church filled this power vacuum, offering a sense of leadership for these bands of people. This church-state, often referred to as Christendom, was headed by the pope. The Catholic church or Christendom wielded much power during this period, as pointed out by the following comment: "Supreme authority was wielded by the pope in the first of these areas and by the emperor in the second" (The Editors of Britannica, 2021). There were some internal struggles within this religious body. Nonetheless, they enjoyed much power throughout this period. Overall, the nomadic lifestyles of these peoples indicated that there was less stability overall in the continent.

Since we are not sure exactly when the movement of these peoples ceased, it is hard to define an exact point in which the early Middle Ages ended. However, generally, the Early Middle Ages is thought to have lasted from 476 to 1000 CE.

THE HIGH MIDDLE AGES

Like with the fall of the Roman Empire that is assumed to have begun with the sack of Rome, the High Middle Ages is argued to have started with a period of stability in the continent, namely the end of Barbarian invasions. Some historians believe that in about 780, the migration of the Germanic peoples ended.

Not only did the invasions end, but the population of Europe increased dramatically and the agricultural boom had proven effective, meaning that more people could leave the rural areas. Urbanization was growing while new empires were emerging. In fact, it was one in particular that brought a type of rebirth—Carolingian Renaissance—to Europe.

Under Charlemagne's rule of the Holy Roman Empire, this rebirth occurred. The construction of schooling and a standardized schooling system, as well as the implementation of Classic Latin, were some of the reforms that Charlemagne brought to Western Europe. Under his leadership, Christendom continued to wield much power over the peoples of Western Europe, but it was a period of growth and stability. The High Middle Ages lasted from 1000 to 1250 CE.

THE LATE MIDDLE AGES

While the High Middle Ages was a period of prosperity and stability, the Late Middle Ages saw an abrupt end to that growth and peace. In other words, it was an era of catastrophe in the continent, where various factors contributed to bring about the crisis and the abrupt halt. First, there was what historians refer to as the "Mini Ice Age." From the early 14th century, the earth experienced a rapid decrease in temperature. Though there are some speculations as to what caused this extreme cooling cycle, it was disastrous for not only Europe but for the Americas and East Russia, too. The dramatically low temperatures meant poor harvests and little food to feed the population. Before the Late Middle Ages, the European population had grown dramatically, but during the Mini Ice Age, having a big population was a huge problem—namely called the Great Famine of 1315 to 1317. It is estimated that 80% of livestock died from disease during this time (Lucas, H.S., 1930). Things only got worse. Second, there were plagues which ravaged the continent. The most obvious example is the Black Death, occurring in 1347. It reached a Sicilian port first and swept through Europe, decimating the population by about 60%. Whatever population growth had been achieved in the Medieval Age was undone in a moment when an infected boat reached the Sicilian Port.

Naturally, the decimation of the European population was devastating, but it brought about terrible consequences for these nations. The Late Middle Ages was prone to social unrest, especially among their peasant parts of the population. Urbanization had also left these individuals in a more vulnerable position, so the peasant revolts that occurred in France and England were also in response to this. Finally, one of the glues that long held Europe in unity had been lost, namely the Western Schism.

In the past, Christianity has experienced many schisms, giving rise to its various denominations. During the Western Schism, there was a dispute as to who was the true pope of the Catholic Church. Three sects emerged all following the leadership of a different pope—one in Pisa, Avignon, and Rome. Still, there were even darker moments experienced in the Late Middle Ages, such as the Crusades and the eventual fall of the Byzantine Empire (Eastern Roman Empire). In fact, the end of the Late Middle Ages has been pinpointed to the moment when Byzantine was lost to the Ottomans, where many civilians fled Eurasia and Asia to seek refuge in Europe. With them, the former Byzantines—and former civilians of Eastern Roman Empire—came aspects of a culture long thought to be dead, yet still very much alive, ushering in the Renaissance—the so-called rebirth of Classical Civilization.

The Late Middle Ages ended with this Renaissance. From 1250 to 1500, it had been a time of catastrophe in Europe. Europe during the Late Middle Ages saw some of its darkest days, certainly with the Black Death, but it was thanks to events in this age that significant achievements were made such as the Protestant Reformation and the fall of Byzantium.

As it stands now, the term "Dark Ages" is no longer appropriate. It is true Europe saw some of its darkest hours during the Middle Ages like the Black Death; catastrophe and crisis occur everywhere, including in great Empires. However, the Middle Ages was not simply a placeholder era. Surely, the first European university in Bologna would not have been created in a continent drenched in barbarism and backwardness. Surely, Europe could not have entered the Age of Exploration without having a solid foundation like the one the Middle Ages had created for its people, like with the agricultural boom and the expansion of industry. In this book, we will explore some of the most fascinating empires that ruled parts of Europe during this era.

CHAPTER TWO

THE HUNNIC EMPIRE

c. 420–469 CE

It is little wonder that fifth-century historians, St. Jerome and St. Patrick, believed that Europe had fallen to ruthless barbarians. With the Germanic bands that traveled into the continent came the Huns, a non-Germanic people and one of the most formidable enemies in all of history. In the fifth century when Atilla came to power, the Huns reached their peak in Europe, and so, the continent saw one of its newest powers emerge. Though the Hunnic empire rose and fell within a century, they have left their mark on history, most notably in the form of their name as the present country of Hungary and the district Hunza in Pakistan.

In this chapter, we will explore the origins of one of the most formidable peoples in Classical and Medieval history. We will then look at their leaders, key events which took place within this empire, and finally, what led to their quick descent.

First Knowledge of the Huns

While some judge the history of the Huns going back as early as 200 BCE, they emerged in Europe as a mysterious group of people. The first contact with the Huns was with the Goths.

The two bands had been living almost side by side, but separated by the straits of Kerch (in Crimea). Despite being in close proximity, the two bands were completely ignorant of the other's presence for some centuries. An incident eventually caused the so-called ice to break.

Two versions of the story exist. One account explains that a cow belonging to a Hunnic herder was stung, causing it to flee to the other side of the Kerch straits. In pursuit of his cow, the herder crossed the straits and encountered the foreign band: the Goths. The other account claims that a Hunnic hunter pursued a stag through the marshes, reaching the other side and making contact with the Goths.

This chance event was great news, as the land across the straits was extremely fertile with a great climate. Unfortunately, it was not great news for the Goths. In 395 CE, the historian Ammianus Marcellinus writes that the Huns were nomadic pastoralists who had no knowledge of agriculture, meaning they migrated regularly in search of fertile land. Across the Kerch straits, there was such rich land for grazing. The only problem was that the land was occupied by the Goths.

Official news of the Huns' existence came to the Romans when scores of displaced Goths moved further inland after the Huns had seized their land. This Hunnic invasion into Gothic territory had a domino effect on the rest of the continent. An Indian source of the time explains this domino effect of the Hun invasion.

> In their search for bread, they drove away by force the people of the country where they found bread. The people thus displaced, proceeded further and drove away the people of the country they occupied. Thus, it was that the Huns had driven away some of the German tribes, who, in their turn, went to other countries. (Modi, J.J., 1917)

As we read, it was the sacking of Rome by the Visigoths that played a crucial role in the fall of the Western Roman Empire. Therefore, the chance encounter that opened the eyes of Hunnic herders or hunters would have far-reaching consequences. On top of this, the Huns' taste for fresh pastures could not be satiated so easily. Once they had made the cross into Europe, they would not stop there.

Who Were the Huns?

While Hunnic reign in Europe may have been short of a century, most historians assume their empire in Asia or Eurasia endured for much longer. Not much is known about the origins of the people who were called the Huns, as their origins are unclear. There is a lack of consensus on their heritage among historians.

To avoid confusion, it should be mentioned that the name 'Huns' was the Latin name for this band of people. Joseph de Guignes, an eighteenth-century historian and authority on the topic, believes the Huns' ancestors were Xiongnu. The Xiongnu would have occupied Mongolia as early as the first century. De Guignes explains that after experiencing a terrible defeat to the Han Dynasty of China, they fled to the Eurasian steppe. De Guignes' suppositions were based on descriptions of the Huns genetic features and culture. From Jordanes, we learn that this band of people had a similar appearance to Mongolians, indicating that the Huns ancestry came from Mongolia.

The problem is that there were a number of tribes living in historical Afghanistan who were called the Iranian Huns. There are others who say that they were a band originally from Kazakhstan.

It gets even more complicated. The Xiongnu did not have a uniform appearance. Rather, they were a political party so their adherents did not have to conform to a genetic pool, making de Guignes' evidence based on the Huns' physical features questionable. However, it does not discredit de Guignes nor other historians who make links to the Iranian Huns. They could have both originated from the Xiongnu, and after the attack from the Chinese Han Dynasty, had fled into Eurasia, Afghanistan, and Mongolia.

Hunnic Culture and Military

The Huns were not farmers, but nomadic pastoralists and hunters. They moved around in search of fertile land for grazing. However, it has been pointed out that up until the Huns movement west into Europe, they had not been completely nomadic. It is true that they moved from area to area, but their migration was confined to the Eurasian Steppe. During Northern Hemisphere summers they settled around the Caspian Sea, but in winter times they migrated to north of the Caspian Sea where the climate was milder.

From the age of three, Hunnic children were taught how to ride a horse. As these people were advanced horse masters, they could move easily from one territory to another. They also lived on game, once again using horses to increase their speed when pursuing their prey.

The Huns primarily were archers—archers who were deadly with a shot. "They were expert archers who used reflex bows made of seasoned birch, bone and glue. Their arrows could strike a man 80 yards away and seldom missed their mark" (History.com Editors, 2018). Second, the formations applied in battle seemed to follow no specific sequence. Rather, they were aimed at confusing their enemies. Lastly, the Huns did not take prisoners. Other bands who successfully conquered other tribes often assimilated the peoples who they were victorious against. This was not the case with the Huns. There were no survivors. It is little wonder that Gibbon called the Huns "the terror of the world" (Modi, J.J., 1917).

The Hunnic Empire

A number of sources indicate that the Hunnic Empire existed before these peoples moved west. According to de Guignes, up until the 1st century, the Hunnic Empire was vast, stretching from the Caspian Sea to China. Nonetheless, by the 1st century, they had lost much of their territory and their empire had become fractured. A whole book can be dedicated to the Xiongnu's empire, but we are solely concerned with the Hunnic Empire in Europe during the Medieval Period.

The Movement West With Balamir

It was in 370 CE when the Romans first became aware of the Huns. A nomadic Iranian group, called the Alans, were conquered by the Huns. Like the Huns, the Alans also conducted warfare on horse. Interestingly enough, the Huns did not kill the survivors in this case, but rather assimilated the Alans. With this extra fighting power, the Huns moved into Gothic territory, waging war against the Ostrogoths in 372. Four years later, they attacked the Visigoths. At the same time, in 376, this band of people were ruled by Balamir (also known as Balamber), who enjoyed a successful reign until 400 CE.

There are two important consequences of this belligerent entrance into Europe. After they "crushed the Ostrogoths," to use the historian Jordanes' wording, they either formed an alliance with Ostrogothic survivors or the now-displaced Ostrogoths were forced to move further inland (Jordanes , n.d.). By assimilating more peoples and warriors, the Hunnic empire expanded. Second, the displacement of the Goths had a domino effect.

The first domino to fall was the Battle of Adrianople which occurred between displaced Goths and Byzantium (1) near Adrianople, now Edirne (northwest Turkey). Even though The Battle of Adrianople took place between the Byzantines and Gothics and Valens, it is considered the first nail in the Roman Empire's coffin (Barbero, A., 2008). Matters did not improve for the Roman Empire. Under Balamir's control, during 395 CE, the Huns began attacking and conquering Roman territories in the Eastern half including Thrace (now a region made up of Turkey, parts of Greece, and Bulgaria), Armenia, and Cappadocia. They seemed unstoppable until a Persian counterattack near Ctesiphon (present-day Baghdad).

Rugila (also Ruas or Ruga), ruling with his brother Octar, successfully led the Hunnic military campaigns in Europe and Eurasia. There were two major outcomes of these European crusades.

First, in 422 CE, when they launched a major attack on Thrace and reached the capital Constantinople, Byzantine leader Theodosius II agreed to an annual tribute to pay for peace between the two nations. Second, prior to this the Huns had been nomadic pastoralists, but with the success of their military campaigns, they settled in the Great Hungarian Plain in Eastern Europe. Thus, the birth of the Hunnic Empire and civilization started in Europe in the early 5th century when this band of nomads established their permanent settlement in the Great Hungarian Plain.

The chapter of the Huns' European civilization had begun. Sadly, while Rugila made this possible, his leadership only lasted for two years. He met his death in about 434 CE.

ATILLA AND BLEDA

Following their uncle Rugila who co-ruled with his brother Octar, the two brothers Atilla and Bleda took the reins of the Hunnic Empire in 432 CE. We know Atilla was born in 406, at a time when the Huns were still initiating their exodus into Eastern Europe.

Atilla and Bleda continued the work their uncle had started. One of their first major acts in the role of Hunnic leaders was to meet their Byzantine counterparts in Margus (in Serbia). Atilla and Bleda met the Byzantine envoys seated on horseback as this was their customary manner of conducting conferences and treaties. The terms were renegotiated; the Huns this time asked for about 660 pounds of gold (216 kg) to be paid as annual tribute (2). Other conditions included territorial claims, increasing the ransom price per prisoner, and opening the Roman market to the Huns.

Such advantageous conditions allowed the Hunnic Empire to flourish. Not only did the Huns have access to more resources from the open markets and annual tribute, but they enjoyed stability under Atilla and Bleda for more than a decade. Still, the Huns aimed to expand their empire. Peace with the Romans brought the Huns into Central Asia again when they invaded the Sassanid Empire (3). However, the Sassanid Empire withstood the invasion from the Huns, in turn bringing the Huns to return to their original ambition—territorial expansion in Europe.

The Sassanids were probably relieved to see the Huns leave their pastures, but not everyone enjoyed the same feelings. In 440 CE, a fresh attack was launched on Byzantium. Though Theodosius II had drawn up a peace treaty against the Huns, in the intervening years, he had strengthened the walls of Constantinople (4). Roman merchants on the northern bank of the Danube became the target of the Hunnish onslaught. They moved into Illyricum and Viminacium (Roman cities in the Balkans).

According to the Huns, what provoked this new onslaught on the Byzantine Empire was that the Bishop of Margus had entered Hunnic territory and looted their royal graves. Atilla and Bleda marched towards Margus with the intention of having the stolen items returned. The bishop evaded capture, but the city fell.

Viminacium, Singidunum (now Belgrade), and numerous other Roman cities in the Balkans were razed to the ground. The Byzantine Empire, this time, was sure of victory against the Huns. Theodosius II, refusing to meet the Huns' new demands, ordered reinforcements from Sicily and invested more gold into the Byzantine army. In the interim, cities in the Balkans were laid to waste and their inhabitants massacred. Buildings continued to be razed as the Huns were armed with battering rams and rolling siege towers. Like most war scenarios, there were few survivors. All the time, fear of the Huns was ever more increasing—they were laying a path straight to Constantinople, the heart of Byzantium. With their new armaments, their battering rams, and rolling siege towers, suddenly the Byzantines were not sure the great walls of Constantinople would hold.

Fortunately for the Romans, they did. However, the Romans were not able to make a positive counterattack. With the Huns unable to penetrate the walls of Constantinople and the Romans unable to make an effective resistance against the Huns, a bloody stalemate ensued.

Without delay, in about 443, Theodosius sent an envoy to negotiate a new peace treaty with the Huns. And as you may guess, the Huns were not lenient. They asked for an immediate payment of 6000 pounds of gold. In addition, the annual tribute would be tripled to 2100 pounds of gold (687 kg) and the price for a Roman prisoner was exorbitantly high. Happy with the terms, the Huns withdrew and Theodosius sighed a breath of relief.

Two years later, Bleda died. The exact circumstances of his death are unknown. There is some reference as to Atilla killing him. Bleda might have been the first to strike his brother, but that is another legend. What we do know is that Atilla became the sole ruler of the Huns.

The Scourge of God

Atilla probably would have been pleased with Gibbon's blasting the Huns as "the terror of the world." After all, the Hunnic leader had proclaimed himself *flagellum Dei*: "the Scourge of God." The Roman Empire had become subject to its own internal decay. In some people's eyes, Atilla was acting on divine authority, punishing the Romans for their decadent and hedonistic lifestyles.

From a modern perspective, this title is more appropriate than most people think. If you consider it in light of the view held by Renaissance thinkers—who believed that the classical civilizations achieved the pinnacle of success for humankind—it is hard to see the Romans as the epitome of human success if their lives were completely devoted to carnal and epicurean pleasure. The title "scourge of God" gives the impression that Attila was a brutal and violent barbarian who acted on the wishes of a violent deity. However, this portrayal may not necessarily reflect the reality of his motivations, being more political than religious, although brutal and violent he certainly was.

In 447, the newly consolidated Hunnic king Attila once again made an attack on Byzantium, targeting the Balkans and Thrace. There are claims that Atilla and the Huns leveled 70 cities during this time.

While Atilla inched towards Constantinople, there were a number of critical changes. First, a plague had broken out in Byzantium. Second, in 450 Marcian took over as emperor from Theodosius II, and he took a hard line against the Huns. The former treaties were revoked ending the annual tribute. In this sense, Marcian was successful against the Huns. They reached Thermopylae (Northern Greece) but soon retreated.

Nevertheless, the Roman Empire was not left alone. An unexpected incident brought Atilla to the Western Roman Empire, its heart being Rome. In 450, Honoria, sister of the Emperor Valentinian III, sent Atilla a ring. Her motives are unknown, but Atilla took it as a sign of her intention to marry him. The opportune leader did not miss his chance to exploit the situation to his advantage and asked Valentinian III for half the Roman Empire as her dowry. Obviously, the Emperor rejected this request. As a result, the terror of the world and the scourge of God marched on the Western Roman Empire—and they were not coming alone.

Atilla managed to recruit the support of the Ostrogoths, Alans, Burgurdians, and a number of Germanic tribes for his army. While the exact number is probably less, the historian Jordanes states that they totalled half a million. A year later, they were in the Roman province of Gaul. And soon commenced one of the most memorable Medieval Battles: the Battle of the Catalaunian Plains.

THE BATTLE OF THE CATALAUNIAN PLAINS

On both sides, there were allegiances. The Visigoths joined the Western Roman Empire as their king had been persuaded by the generalissimo, Flavius Aetius.

The Battle of the Catalaunian Plains is one of the most famous in medieval history. There are several reasons for this, one being that it was a major conflict. The Hunnic Empire had grown in size, dominating much of Eastern Europe and Eurasia. While they are not sure what the death toll was, there are estimates from 40,000 to 300,000. In a world already fraught with famine, plague, and disease, 40,000 men dying was massive. It was also an incredibly tactical fight. According to some sources, combat only began at 14:30 in the afternoon, as it took the whole morning for the leaders to deploy their coalitions and legions.

Though the Battle of the Catalaunian Plains is recognized as one of the most memorable scenes of conflict in history; there is a lot of uncertainty regarding what exactly took place. First, the location is unknown or debated. There is some consensus among historians that Atilla and the Huns—with the invasion into Gaul—had reached Orleans before Aetius, flanked by the Visigoths, put a stop in their tracks. What is known is that Aetius, from the ages of 14 to 17, lived among the Huns where he was kept as a hostage. In fact, it was this friendship with Aetius that prevented the Huns from attacking the Western Roman Empire in former times, as Aetius was the most powerful—or at least, the second most powerful—person in the empire (5). Thus, Aetius had familiarity with Hunnic culture and military strategies.

What is known is that the Battle of the Catalaunian Plains ended in a Hunnic defeat and victory for the Roman-Visigoth coalition. Initially, the Huns had the upper hand as the Visigoth center in the coalition's formation was defeated quite soon after the fighting commenced.

However, the legions, cavalry, and archers flanking the Roman-Visigoth coalition were too strong for the Huns and their allies. When defeat was imminent, the Huns fled the scene, but strangely Aetius did not follow. The exact reason is not known. It could have been owing to an old loyalty to the Huns or receiving a bribe from Atilla. Despite this missed opportunity, the Romans were victorious. Edward Gibbon explains that the Battle of the Catalaunian Plains was the last West Roman triumph before its demise. On the other hand, the Battle of the Catalaunian Plains was one of the first defeats the Huns had suffered against the Romans.

Invasion of Italy

Atilla did not give up his ambitions of marrying Honoria and claiming half of the Empire for her dowry. In 452, he renewed his attempt, but this time, he took another route. Instead of taking the route through Gaul, he went directly for Italy. Like with his previous campaign, numerous cities such as Venice were captured and Aquileia (near Venice) were destroyed.

This time, Atilla's attempts were more successful as he reached Rome. Pope Leo, residing in Rome at the time, met with Atilla. A second strange incident occurred: Atilla did not proceed with his marriage to Honoria. He with his entourage simply spared the Western Romans further onslaught. Like with the first mysterious occurrence—Aetius' decision not to pursue the Huns—there are several theories. One is that Pope Leo convinced Atilla not to advance into Rome as a plague had spread through the population, and if the Huns had gone ahead with their plans, they would have become its next victims. Another postulation is that the Western Roman Empire was considerably weak—much weaker than its Eastern counterpart. Famine and starvation had emptied much of the granaries. It would not have been worthwhile for the Huns to continue with the march into Rome. Finally, and probably the most absurd theory, is that Pope Leo appealed to Atilla's good conscience, and that it was morality that saved the Romans. Whatever the reason, the Huns were gone and Rome was spared.

Death of Atilla and Hunnic Decline

Unlike many other military leaders and heroes, Atilla did not die a warrior's death. As you have seen up to now, there is a lot of speculation around significant events like the death of Bleda. The same applies to the death of Atilla, who died on his wedding night after suffering a nosebleed in March 453. There are several main theories.

The first is that it was a freak accident. Atilla drank heavily and feasted late into the night of his wedding night, causing the nosebleed and some kind of stupor, which further brought on Atilla choking on his blood to his death. The second theory is that his recently betrothed wife, Ildico, had poisoned him or used some other means to kill him. Finally, there is some hint that Marcian of the Byzantine empire had secretly planned this assassination of Atilla. Finally, it has also been suggested that the nosebleed was a sign of a hemorrhage as a result of internal bleeding.

Whatever the cause of Atilla's death, without their strong leader, the empire was left to the king's three sons. With power no longer consolidated under one figure, the oldest son, Ellak, ruled over Akatziri while the second eldest son, Dengizich, led the Western Huns. At the same time, Turkic and Eurasian tribes were moving into Hunnic territory in the Eurasian Steppe, threatening the stability of the Huns in that region. A clear indication that there was division among the Huns was in 467 when Dengizich launched another attack on the Romans without the support of his youngest brother—Atilla's third son, Ernak. Two years later, Dengizich's military campaign ended in defeat and he met his death in the same year in Thrace. Dengizich's death seemed to bring on the dissolution of the Hunnic empire, as it is generally believed this band of people were assimilated into a nomadic Turkic tribe called the Bulgars.

The Huns will be forever doomed to the label 'barbarians.' While it is true that they were one of the fiercest, deadliest, and most ruthless of warriors, their success on the battlefield is not a consequence of being bloodthirsty barbarians. It was rather thanks to their mastery of archery and disarming warfare strategies. They are certainly known for their military prowess and strength. Even now, their reputation as being one of the fiercest fighters lives on. What they are less known for is their extensive Hunnic empire stretching from the Eurasian steppe to the Danube Valley in Eastern Europe across to France. Though the Hunnic Empire existed just short of 50 years, it was the first to contend with that of the Romans and the first of the Medieval Period.

CHAPTER THREE

THE KINGDOM OF THE LOMBARDS

c. 568–774 CE

T he Hunnic Empire has disintegrated. Rome had fallen. Byzantium made claims to the former Roman territories, but stirring in Eastern Europe, a new power came to contest the Byzantines for those fallen regions.

In this section, we will cover the Lombards, a Germanic tribe who for two centuries ruled much of Italy. While their reign was marked by political instability, insurrection, and medieval espionage, we will analyze how the Lombards brought Italy under their rule despite these numerous adversities. In this chapter, we will review the rise and fall of the Lombards.

Conditions for a New Kingdom

Soon after the Hunnic Empire dissolved, the Western Roman Empire met its own demise. Byzantium remained intact. Its Emperor, Justinian I, planned to restore the Roman Empire to its former condition. *Renovatio imperii Romanorum*—meaning renewal of the empire of the Romans—was Justinian I's plan for Byzantium to extend its imperial reach into Italy. However, the Byzantines were not counting on a new force emerging in Italy—namely, the Lombards.

After the fall of the Western Roman Empire, war-torn Italy was the perfect breeding ground for invasion. Typically, whenever a revolution occurs or a group of governance is removed, a power vacuum is created. A natural consequence is for that void to be filled—generally, by the next leader, general, or force that has the strongest will to do so. Though the Byzantines had moved into parts of Italy, these former Roman territories in Italy were so devastated by famine (1) and plague (2) that the Lombards easily annexed them, thereby creating their own kingdom.

After Justinian I's death, his nephew Justin II was crowned Byzantine emperor in 565. While his uncle was known for his attempts at restoring the Roman Empire to its former glory, Justin II's reign is marked by his loss of Italy. In 568, three years later, the Lombards started their conquest of Italy.

Origins of the Lombards and Lombardian Culture

One of the tribes joining the Migration Period were the Lombards. They, along with other Germanic tribes like the Suebi, lived in the Elbe Rhine River region, approximately made of Germany and Czech Republic in modern times. However, this tribe split up to find new territories. With this design, this band of people encountered the Vandals who gave them an ultimatum: to go to war or pay tribute. This Germanic tribe took the harder option, which, ironically led to the birth of their name. Paul the Deacon—a historian living in the eighth century renowned for his work *The History of the Lombards*—explains the origins of the name Lombard.

> When the Vandals were ready to meet their counterparts in combat, the Lombards got their women to march with their men, tying their hair around their chins to create the false impression that they were men. It was an intimidation technique. From that moment, they were called "Longobards" translating to 'longbeards.' Overtime, the form changed and soon the term Lombard arose (Melandsø, n.d.).

After the Suebi tribe split up, the Lombards went further inland in search of territory. This brought them to Pannonia (now western Hungary). Until the fifth century, the Romans ceded control of this region to the Huns. Though it is not exactly known when the Lombards moved into Pannonia, it is assumed to have occurred during the late fourth century. At this stage, the Romans still controlled Pannonia. The Lombards formed an alliance with the Romans and both fought against the Ostrogoths. Despite the alliance, Roman culture had little influence on the Lombards.

One of the most infamous traits of the Lombards was their divergence in religious beliefs. Both Byzantium and the Western Roman Empire enjoyed a mass conversion to Catholicism. This was especially true in Byzantium. Justinian I played a critical role for introducing a number of religious regulations. When this emperor went forward with *Renovatio imperii Romanorum*, Rome was a key location—remaining a papal state for many centuries. The Lombards were either adherents of Arian Christianity or they were pagans. It is difficult to explain the exact divergence in belief between Arianism and Catholicism, but the Arians did not subscribe to the concept of a Holy Trinity. Interestingly, it was this difference in religious adherence that played a crucial role in the events that were to come.

The Kingdom and Duchies of the Lombards

For almost two decades, the Byzantines fought the Ostrogoths during the Gothic War. When the Lombards, under their King Albion, entered northern Italy during this time, their invasion went almost unopposed. They crossed the Julian Alps (in Austria and Italy). The first city the Lombards claimed was Forum Iulii (now Cividale del Friuli, one of Italy's most north-eastern towns, on the border of Slovenia). By 569, they had added nearly all the principal northern cities to their kingdom except Pavia, a city about 22 miles south of Milan. After three years, the Lombards eventually conquered Pavia, establishing it as their capital.

They did not stop there. They moved into central and southern parts of the peninsula, creating Longobardia Major, composed of the Northern territories, and Longobardia Minor, comprising the southern and central territories. Up to then, the Lombards had accomplished what no other tribe had achieved. They had managed to break the political unity of the Italian peninsula. Since the Roman conquest of Italy more than eight centuries ago, the peninsula remained under one central control. Now, with the Lombards in Italy, there were regions belonging to the Lombards as well as those still in the hands of Byzantines. It was the clearest sign that the Western Roman Empire had truly ended.

In the meantime, Byzantium still retained control over some territories in Italy, named the Exarchate of Ravenna. Another Exarchate also existed at the time: the Exarchate of Africa. These regions were under the control of the exarch, a type of governor who took orders from Byzantium. What this implies is that this governor, the exarch, had an incredible amount of power in the province of Italy. According to Stefano Gasparri, the formation of the exarchate seemed to occur largely in response to the Lombard conquest in Italy. The Byzantines were trying to build up a strong enough military defense to stop the Lombards from annexing regions of Italy.

In contrast, administration of the Lombard Kingdom could not have been more different. As territories continued to be claimed, the kingdom continued to grow. Albion created 39 duchies, each headed by its own duke. Each duchy enjoyed much autonomy, making the kingdom lack any real cohesion overall. Throughout the existence of this kingdom, dukes would make their own claims to the throne, even if it meant betrayal. For example, in the early 8th century, coups were particularly common. Furthermore, betrayal—as a means of bringing political success—often entailed working with the kingdom's main adversary, the Byzantine empire, who wished nothing more than for the Lombard kingdom to fall. Though some were established after the initial conquest, Thomas Hodgkin, in his book *Italy and her Invaders*, reveals the four most powerful duchies were the duchies of Tridentum and Friuli in Longobardia Major and the duchies of Benevento and Spoleto in Longobardia Minor.

After Albion died in 572, the idea was for the dukes to congregate to elect their new king. While each duke enjoyed much rule of his own, this soon became a problem itself as the individual dukes had too much power, creating instability.

Internal Problems and Collusion

Byzantium was not quite ready to hand over Italy to the Lombards. There were two major reasons why the Byzantines opposed Lombard rule in Italy. First, because it was Italy—and as we have already read, it was the most significant territory in the Roman Empire. Second, there was a religious difference. The Byzantines were Roman Catholics. The Lombards, initially, were not. They subscribed to Arianism or Paganism. Therefore, the Byzantines had two principal motivations for wishing the Lombard empire to fail.

It was in 582 that Byzantium set up the Exarchate of Ravenna, with the sole goal of reclaiming the regions from the Lombards. This was against the will of the people as it meant sending them into conflict once more, now against the Lombards. We have already discussed the appalling conditions in Italy during the time. Honestly, the last thing the population wanted was further conflict. Joshua Mark, a contemporary historian who specializes in Ancient History, gives more insight.

> The Exarchs were military commanders whose role would be to organize the populace and equip an army. The people of Italy, however, who still remembered the exorbitant taxes of the empire, were not interested in seeing a return of imperial rule and had even less interest in seeing their tax money go to finance more wars of the empire instead of going to improvements in their own land. The Exarchate, therefore, was ineffective and came to nothing (Mark, J.J., 2014).

As the initial means of Byzantine proved unsuccessful, they had to devise a new strategy to vanquish the Lombards.

Murder and Coup D'état

What is known is that there was a plot to have Albion killed. The king's wife, Rosamund, formed some kind of deal with Helmichis, Albion's foster brother and bodyguard. He proved nothing but a turncloak with far greater ambitions. The assassination was successful. On June 28, Albion's wife arranged Albion's killing with the help of a servant. Paul the Deacon hints at a servant not being involved, which means that it was Rosamund and Helmichis conspiring to assassinate Albion. There is some speculation that the Byzantine empire may have also been involved.

Though it is uncertain whether Byzantium went as far as to murder Albion, there is little doubt that they had a hand in orchestrating the coup d'état that followed. Helmichis married Rosamund and made a vie for the throne. Their ambitions were supported by the Byzantines, seeking to move the capital to Verona. Rosamund, as a Gepid (3), could count on the Gepid garrison in Verona. If Rosamund and Helmichis were successful, the already divided Lombard Kingdom would be further fractured with the loss of Verona.

Rosamund and Helmichis' plans failed, despite Rosamund's intentions for killing Albion to get revenge over the death of her father, Cunimund, whom Albion had killed in 567. Rosamund's taste for vengeance is understandable. After Albion killed Cunimund, in line with Lombard tradition, Albion made a drinking cup from his skull. Despite her understandable intentions for murdering Albion, the population did not side with her. Conspiracy with Byzantium was evident. After the coup d'état fell through, Helmichis and Rosamund fled to Ravenna, where eventually, the two lovers in exile killed each other. Subsequently, the Lombard dukes elected a new king, Cleph.

THE EMPIRE STRIKES BACK

In 572, Cleph was crowned king of the Lombards. Following in his predecessor's shoes, Cleph immediately aimed to expand the kingdom. The new king enjoyed much success as the whole of Italy's northern territory fell under the rule of the Lombards; Tuscany too was annexed. Moreover, Lombard land had grown so much that it now extended to the gates of Ravenna, gaining on the Byzantines. There is little known of Cleph except that he was an immensely intimidating and frightening character who was of no blood link to Albion. Having no blood ties reveals the unique structure of the Lombard kingdom. To become king means you had to be elected by the dukes.

Despite being able to colonize the whole of Northern Italy, Cleph's reign ended 18 months later. In 574, Cleph became the second victim of regicide. His slave killed him. Once again, it has been hinted that the Byzantines were also involved in this assassination.

Following Cleph's death, a new king was not voted in by the dukes and the kingdom experienced a decade's long *interregnum*—meaning each duchy obtained full-autonomy. The ruling dukes with their families were completely independent. As mentioned, members of the Roman aristocracy were the victims of the Lombards invasion in Italy. During the *interregnum*, this occurred on a greater scale. As the dukes wished to replace the former lineages dominant in various cities and provinces, they made to extinguish previous lines of aristocracy or royalty. With the noble families removed, the dukes with their families enjoyed even greater power in each duchy. The 10-year *interregnum* also fractured the Lombard Kingdom. As each duke's power grew, the kingdom became more divided. This was certainly playing right into the hands of the Byzantines.

Centralized Monarchy

It soon became clear to these dukes that the more power they had individually, the weaker the overall Lombard Kingdom, making it more vulnerable to an attack from the Byzantines or Franks. As you will remember, it was during 582 that the Exarchate of Ravenna was officially formed. During the *interregnum*, there were a number of events which resulted in the Lombard Kingdom being susceptible to attack.

In 574 to 575, the Lombards had extended their own reach into Provence in Southeast France. They were now encroaching on a territory that belonged to an established kingdom, namely the Kingdom of Burgundy belonging to the Merovingian dynasty. This attack on Merovingian territory provoked an assault on Northern Italy. The situation had become even worse for the Lombards as encroaching on French land brought the Byzantines and French into an alliance. Just simply having a common enemy was enough for the two nations. Thus, with the Lombards weaker than ever to an attack from the Franks or Exarchate, they realized the necessity of having a unified kingdom. In 584, Cleph's son, Authari, was elected king. After being crowned king, the dukes ceded half of their property to indicate the necessity of having a more centralized monarchy.

Authari's reign was marked by conflict with the Franks, Byzantines, and Lombard rebels. The rebellion of the Duke Droctulf of Broscello in Emilia-Romagna was emblematic of the lack of internal political stability. Fortunately, Authari was able to suppress this insurrection, even if Droctulf had sought an alliance with the Byzantines.

Facing conflict on several frontiers with the Franks and Byzantines did not stop Authari from expanding the kingdom's borders and taking the last stronghold of the Byzantines in Como. Under Authari, things were looking up for the Lombards. In 585, Authari and the Lombards survived an attack from the Franks. By doing so, he also negotiated a truce with the Byzantines. It is not that the Lombards defeated their French rivals; it is rather that they avoided going to war. Authari simply locked himself away in his Pavia stronghold and the soldiers simply did not meet the Franks for combat. Nonetheless, a truce with the Byzantines was achieved. Outright war was avoided.

To establish peace with the Franks, Authari arranged to marry a Frankish princess. It is not known exactly why the marriage did not take place, but it did not. While marriage between the French and Lombard houses would have ensured peace, Authari's next step was decisive, bringing the Kingdom a century of war with the Franks. He married the Bavarian princess, Theodelinda, instead. The Bavarians were the Franks' natural enemies. For the Lombards, Theodelinda held much importance, as her heritage linked to past Lombard royalty. Such a union allowed royal blood lines to re-enter the monarchy.

Though the partnership with Theodelinda brought out the French wrath, it also led to Theodelinda becoming more involved in the rule of the kingdom. Not only was she a respected leader, but she was a Catholic. She encouraged her husband to adopt more Catholic practices and to encourage the practice of Catholicism in the kingdom.

As mentioned, the Frankish rage was awakened. In 590, Authari was able to withstand French attacks again. He soon met his death after being poisoned. Though war with the Franks was constant, it was under Authari that the Lombards began to enjoy a period of internal stability.

Agilulf and Theodelinda

The political stability that had begun with Authari continued with Agilulf. In 590, Agilulf, the duke of Turin, took to the throne. It was at Theodelinda's recommendation that Agilulf be crowned king. As Queen Theodelinda was much respected among the Turin people, and came from royal Lombard descent, Agilulf asked for her hand in marriage so that her influence in the kingdom could continue.

Like Authari, it was Theodelinda's religious adherence which too influenced Agilulf to get baptized. This drew some criticism from Lombard citizens, but this did little to dissuade the King. When his son, Adaloald, was born he too was baptized, and Catholic monasteries were erected—the most famous being the Cathedral of Monza, dedicated to St. John the Baptist.

Before Authari died, the French were planning their next assault. Agilulf took immediate action to negotiate peace with the Franks and also to fortify the Lombard frontiers. In a special turn of events, the King of Burgundy died in 592 and the Franks descended into civil war. This allowed Agilulf and Theodelinda to focus on things back at home. The Lombards continued with their expansion into the Exarchate's territories. In 602, the Byzantines decisively lost Padua and, two years later, Mantua and Cremona. Moreover, Agilulf realized that the power of each duke was destabilizing the kingdom. He and his wife took measures to limit their power by installing a royal official in each duchy. Even more property was annexed by Agilulf.

Agilulf's reign continued till 616, twenty-six years in total. Compared to his predecessors who ruled for less than a decade, Agilulf's long reign indicated stability within the kingdom. After capturing Padua, the Lombards forced the Exarchate to pay tribute. With fortified borders, internal stability, and a neutralized Exarchate, Agilulf lived out the last decade of his reign in peace. While Agilulf was certainly an excellent leader, Theodelinda also played a pivotal role. First, it had been on her recommendation that Agilulf was chosen as king. She also contributed to the end of the war in Rome between the Papacy and the Lombards. Even before Agilulf was named king, Theodelinda was respected among her people for being an effective leader. If you have any doubts, on his deathbed Agilulf asked for her to act as regent while their son Adaloald matured for the role. Though Agilulf enjoyed a 26-year long reign, Theodelinda was queen and regent for a total of 35 years.

Return to Turmoil and Political Disintegration

The work of Theodelinda and Agilulf had ushered in continued internal political stability. Yet when Adaloald came of age and succeeded to the throne, he succumbed to insanity.

The next two rulers enjoyed some stability as Arioald, who took over in 626, ruled for a decade, while his successor Rothari had a reign that spanned 16 years. Not everything that Agilulf had implemented was maintained by these dukes when they took over. For instance, Arioald was an Arian and did not accept the newly welcomed Catholicism. Unlike Arioald, Rothari was tolerant of Catholics, putting him in line for the throne after Arioald died. One of the main achievements of Arioald was that he successfully repelled an attack from the Avars, a band of Eurasian nomads, on the northeast border. There is more information available on what Rothari accomplished during his tenure.

It was with Rothari that the Lombards annexed the remaining territories from the Exarchate. Their holdings were limited to a few provinces. Another historic moment was the creation of Edictum Rothari, which was a code of Lombard Law. The edict was written in Vulgar Latin, demonstrating that Romanisation had taken place within the Lombard kingdom. After Rothari's death, his son, Rodoald succeeded him. Six months later, an act of regicide tainted the Lombard kingdom again as Rodoald was killed by a fellow Lombard for philandry.

And soon, the original curse of short-lived tenures began to plague the Lombards again. For almost a century, few monarchs of Lombard held the throne for longer than a decade. To make matters worse, the Lombard kingdom seemed doomed to suffer the same fate as the Roman Empire, splitting the empire into two. The capital remained at Pavia, but a second one was established at Milan in 653. Internal disintegration was the cause for this continued disruption to leadership. It was only in 744 that matters improved.

Decline of the Lombards

When Liutprand was crowned king in 744, it seemed unlikely that the Lombard kingdom would not survive to the next century. Though Agilulf and Rothari had contributed much to the internal stability in the kingdom, Joshua Mark remarks that Liutprand is considered the greatest Lombard ruler after Albion. One of the achievements this excellent ruler managed was an alliance with the Franks, as Liutprand pledged loyalty to Charles Martel. Joshua Mark also reveals that there were several wars with the Byzantines and Lombards under Liutprand's reign, but in the majority of cases, the Lombards were successful. Another significant feat of Liutprand's tenure was negotiation with the Papacy, known as the Donation of Sutri. The significant region Latium and Sutri composed part of the agreement between Pope Leo II and Liutprand, which involved Liutprand handing over these areas to the Papacy. Overall, the turmoil of former decades seemed to be forgotten with Liutprand, and as Joshua Mark indicates about Liutprand's time in power: "His reign was characterized by security and prosperity" (Mark, J.J, 2014).

The last king was Desiderius, a royal officer in the duchy of Tuscany. Following Aiustulf's turbulent and violent leadership, even the Papacy and Franks supported Desiderius' ascendance to the throne. Desiderius experienced much resistance from the two great duchies in Longobardia minor, Spoleto and Benevento. Though Liutprand was able to quell resistance earlier in these duchies, decades later Desiderius encountered a similar rebellion from Spoleto. Ironically, an upstart also named Liutprand had ambitions for greater power in the Duchy. One of Desiderius' achievements was to quash the rebellion and bring Spoleto under his control. Whereas Liutprand, the former king, built an alliance with both the Papacy and Byzantines, Desiderius seemed to undermine Liutprand's work. The Donation of Sutri handed significant land over to the pope. After visiting the tomb of St. Peter, Desiderius went ahead with his plans to extend the Lombard Kingdom, even if it meant seizing Papal territories. Once again he sought help from Byzantium, with the possible plot of deposing all papal authority. Naturally, such a plan was welcomed by the Byzantines. Fortunately for the Papacy, they had a strong ally in the Franks, and their Frankish leader was the legendary Charlemagne. Living up to his name, Charlemagne sent two Frankish armies in 773. After eight months, Pavia fell. The king and the capital were captured and, as abruptly as that, the kingdom of the Lombards ended.

The Italian peninsula has suffered numerous invasions by the Huns, Ostrogoths, Franks, and the Lombards. However, only the Lombards managed to leave a lasting imprint of their reign on the country. Today, Lombardia is the region of Milan, Italy's industrial & financial capital, and numerous other important cities such as Pavia, Monza, and Bergamo. That is not the only memorabilia left by the Lombards. Their family name has traveled the world. Their bloodlines are yet to end. Theirs was a kingdom that rose in the vacancy of the Western Roman Empire. In some sense, they were an excellent substitute as they managed to stave off attacks from various enemies for two centuries. Their road to the creation of their kingdom may have been an easy one, but their path to maintaining rule over the Italian peninsula was riddled with war, medieval conspiracy, and internal political instability.

CHAPTER FOUR

THE UMAYYAD CALIPHATE

c. 661–750 CE

W hile the Byzantines had their hands full with the Lombards and Sassanid Empire in the 7th and 8th centuries, forces were at work in the Arabian Peninsula. The death of the Prophet Mohammed was the catalyst for a wave of change. For almost a century, the whole of Arabia was consolidated into the domain of one empire, but there was a hefty price to pay: bloody civil wars known as the Four Fitnas, insurrection, and brutal suppression. Despite the internal dissent and dissidence, the Umayyad Caliphate was the only Arabian dynasty to reign over all of Arabia at one time. Theirs was an empire that expanded from Portugal to Pakistan. This was the success of Umayyad Caliphate, bringing all of Arabia and further to accept the rule of Islam.

In this chapter, we will discuss how the Umayyad Caliphate consolidated the whole of Arabia into one empire, how they continued to expand the empire's dominion, and how the internal dissent was ever a thorn in the dynasty's side.

Background to the Caliphate's Formation

On June 8th, 632, the Prophet Mohammed died from what is believed to be Medinan fever. Apart from creating the faith of Islam, Mohammed also played a pivotal role in history. With the creation of Islam, the Prophet united the whole of the Arabia into a single polity. As Mohammed's following grew in the 7th century, this new change—the creation of Islam—faced much opposition while the religion was in its infancy.

There were numerous opponents of Islam, but Mohammed's principal adversary was Abu Sufyan, head of the Umayyad Clan—the most powerful family. The growing influence of Islam was a threat to the Umayyad Clan's power. Nonetheless, even members of this clan such as Abu Sufyan and his son, Muawiya I, converted to Islam. While Mohammed's leadership united all of Arabia, his death brought much division among his followers.

In the wake of his death, four individuals took over Mohammed's role as leader. These individuals are known as the Rightly Guided Caliphates, or *Rashidun*, consisting of Abū Bakr, 'Umar, 'Uthmān, and Alī. With four leaders, the question is, who rules? The answer is all of them, but it was not as simple as that—for the disciples or companions to Mohammed, known as *anṣār*, also held enormous political influence. Britannica provides more insight: "[F]or his successors, and a large and influential body of anṣār (companions of the Prophet) kept close watch on the caliphs to ensure their strict adherence to divine revelation (the Qur'ān) and the Sunnah" (The Editors of Britannica, 2020). Therefore, even from the beginning, the *Rashidun* had limited power and had to acquiesce to the demands of the *anṣār*. Overtime, this would lead to the breakdown of the *Rashidun*.

Mohammed's closest advisor and father-in-law, Abū Bakr, was elected the first leader of the *Rashidun* caliphate, which controlled all of Arabia in 632. For the next two years, Abū Bakr ruled. However, Abū Bakr's reign was fraught with rebellion. Many of the tribes in the Arabian Peninsula—with the exception of those in Mecca and Medina—renounced their faith or stopped paying the customary religious tax of Alms. With the risk of the region becoming divided again and undoing Mohammed's work, Abū Bakr engaged in the Ridda Wars for the next year. From Northern Saudi Arabia to Yemen, the Rashidun caliphate under Abū Bakr's leadership engaged in warfare to keep the Islamic peoples united. The Rashidun caliphate won every war, maintaining control of the Arabian Peninsula.

Abū Bakr hoped to extend the Caliphate's reach into Persia and the Levant (1), but in 634, he fell ill with fever and died on August 23. 'Umar was named the next Caliphate, but his reign ended abruptly when he was assassinated during morning prayers in 644. 'Umar's advisors then voted 'Uthmān to be the next caliphate. However, it should be noted that three of his six advisors were from the Quraysh, affiliated with the Umayyad clan.

'Uthmān enjoyed the longest reign as Rashidun caliphate. It was in the latter years of his rule that stability was threatened. Despite the protests, 'Uthmān managed to expand the empire into North Africa and parts of Europe, but a mob of angry protestors broke into his house and killed him in 656. There has been some suggestion that 'Uthmān's death was the result of a conspiracy. When Ali, the fourth Rightly Guided Caliphate, became the next caliph, his rule was soon interrupted by 'Uthmān followers who wished for the leader's death to be avenged. 'Uthmān's nephew, Muawiya I, was particularly adamant. Ali, however, failed to respond and take vengeance. Muawiya I and other like-minded followers declared war on Ali. What ensued was civil war, consisting of a series of battles. The Battle of Camel saw Muawiya I as the new caliph with Ali deposed.

The Emergence and Culture of the Umayyad Caliphate

Originally, when the Prophet Mohammed was still the leader of the Islamic following, he made peace with his original opponents, including those of the Umayyad Clan, by making them governors over certain territories. In the case of Muawiya I, he was given the role of Syria. Since his power base was in Syria, when he took over in 661, he moved the capital of the Umayyad Caliphate—now supplanting the Rashidun caliphate—to Damascus. From there he ruled. One key aspect that made the Umayyad Caliphate different from the Rashidun one was that it became a hereditary role, meaning that Muawiya I could pass the title down to his son after his death. As we will see later, it was this dynastic form of rule that fractured the Umayyad kingdom.

Despite the fact that it was a civil war (First Fitna) that allowed for Muawiya I to depose Ali, Muawiya I preferred to rule through diplomacy as opposed to war. One such example is after Ali was removed; his son Hasan was elected as the next Caliph. Muawiya I negotiated a peace treaty with Hasan. Syed Muhammad Khan explains how the first Umayyad leader managed such, stating: "He convinced Hasan (l. 624-670 CE), the son of Ali, who had succeeded him in Kufa, to abdicate in his favor in exchange for a high pension" (Khan, S. M., 2020). It was under Muawiya I, the first Umayyad Caliphate, that leadership became more centralized—orders given from Damascus.

Since Muawiya I was interested in maintaining diplomatic ties, he welcomed Christians, especially those from Byzantium. One main motivation behind this was to allow his empire to adopt the administrative and financial systems practiced in Byzantine. This allowed for his empire to run more smoothly and become more economically advanced. What is interesting is that Muawiya I planned to eventually extend the Caliphate into Byzantium. According to the Saylor Foundation, "his ultimate goal was Constantinople" (The Saylor Foundation., n.d.).

As the Umayyad Caliphate grew, culture developed under its various rulers. For example, when Muawiya I ruled, Byzantium administrative and financial systems were adopted. Later, Arabic was adopted as an official language, used for commercial and bureaucratic purposes.

Important landmarks today also were constructed by the Umayyad dynasty including "Desert Castles," bathhouses, hunting lodges, and urban palaces. Additionally, famous plans to construct mosques such as the Dome of the Rock in Jerusalem and the Great Mosque in Cordoba (Spain) were undertaken. This interest in art also extended to frescos and friezes. For instance, in the Museum for Islamic Art in Berlin there is the Mshatta façade dated mid-8th century, which is a splendid design from the Umayyad dynasty. There are also examples of statues and mosaics that come from the time of this Caliphate.

The Expansion of the Empire

MUAWIYA I

The Umayyad Caliphate had its eyes on extending into Byzantium. For a while there were some diplomatic ties between the two empires, but once the civil wars in the Caliphate ceased, the Umayyads turned their attention to Constantinople and attempted to invade it. The Byzantines did not only have to worry about the Arabs from the Caliphate, but also aggression with the Sassanid Empire. In fact, it is possible that the consistent conflict between the Sassanid and Byzantine depleted the militaries and economies of these empires, allowing for the rapid expansion of the Caliphate. After Muawiya I's failed plan to annex Constantinople, he turned to diplomacy. He agreed to pay them annual tributes to ensure peace.

Another reason for the empire's extending its reach so quickly was owing to the terrain. The majority of the countries conquered initially—even under the Rashidun caliphate—were located in the Arabian Peninsula, the Levant, Persia, and North Africa, meaning their terrain was composed of massive expanses of desert which were sparsely populated. These factors allowed for a quick invasion and take over by the Umayyad Caliphate.

One of the means of ensuring stability in the Caliphate was the use of personal bodyguards. Muawiya I had already seen his uncle suffer a political assassination. While the Umayyads were held in high regard in Syria and Mecca, there were apostates and heretics (2) who would seize the opportunity to strike him down. Under Muawiya I, the empire expanded into modern-day Pakistan and Afghanistan to the east, the coast of Morocco to the west, and recovered territories previously lost to Byzantium in the north. In 680, Muawiya I died.

Yazid I

When the Caliphate assumed a hereditary structure, it shook the core of the empire. Before his death, Muawiya I named his son Yazid I as his successor. Noting that ibn means 'son of' in Arabic naming convention, Syed Khan provides more insight:

> The Arabs were not accustomed to dynastic rule and so Yazid's accession was met with much resentment, most notably from Husayn ibn Ali (l. 626-680 CE), Hasan's younger brother, and Abdullah ibn Zubayr (l. 624-692 CE), who was the son of a close companion of Prophet Muhammad (Khan, S. M., 2020).

Muawiya I may have successfully defeated Ali and negotiated peace with his son Hasan, but his actions cast a dark shadow on the empire, especially with Yazid I being crowned caliph.

Under Husayn ibn Ali's instruction, a band of dissidents marched to Damascus, with the intention of ending the Umayyad Caliphate. Yazid was prepared to meet them in combat, and so the Second Fitna began. The Battle of Karbala (modern-day Iraq) saw the creation of the Shi'at Ali Muslims—a group of political rivals who supported Ali, the fourth *Rashidun*. This band intended to overthrow the Umayyad dynasty in Iraq by implementing a lockdown in the city. Husayn ibn Ali's followers met Yazid's forces in Karbala. Husayn was killed in the combat.

Things did not improve for Yazid I. Insurrection occurred in Medina. A political rival originally from Mecca, Ibn al-Zubayr, gained support for his ambitions of deposing Yazid in Medina. Yazid I harshly quashed the rebellions in both Medina and Mecca, tainting these cities forever with a brutal and violent reaction. It was not only Yazid's brutal response to the insurrection but also the siege of his political opponents that led to such a brutal imprint on the cities.

It was not only in Mecca and Medina where Yazid I did not have much luck. His expansions in North Africa provoked the retaliation of the Berbers, causing revolts in the cities of Tangier and Volubilis in Morocco. His campaign to seize land from the Byzantines, once again an attempt for Constantinople, ended in failure. All in all, Yazid I had undone some of the work of his father. Khan sheds more light on the period under Yazid, indicating:

> Today Yazid is remembered as perhaps the most negative figure in Islamic history. His son Muawiya II (r. 683-684 CE) was proclaimed caliph after his death, but the sickly youngster wanted no share in his father's ill actions (Khan, S. M., 2020).

MARWAN I

In 683, Yazid I met his demise. He, like his father, succumbed to illness. For the subsequent two years, the Umayyad Caliphate failed to produce a successful leader. Yazid I named his son, Mu'awiya II, as his successor. In 684, Mu'awiya II died from what is believed to be jaundice. Things got even worse. Ibn al-Zubayr declared himself the new Caliphate and it seemed that the Umayyad dynasty was likely to end, for Mu'awiya II had not named a successor.

Marwan I, an Umayyad loyal to Yazid I who helped end the insurrection in Medina, volunteered himself. Naturally, there was some dissent to this among the advisors in Syria. Marwan I took the necessary steps to rightfully put himself forward the title, including marrying Yazid's widow. What is known is that he eventually was granted this title as 9th-century historian, al-Ya'qubi, reveals in his writings that Marwan I swore to take vengeance upon Uthman and continue the work of the Umayyads.

On June 22nd, 684 he was crowned Caliph. About six to ten months later, he died. While his reign was incredibly short, Marwan I ensured the Umayyad Caliphate's survival by volunteering himself for the role.

ABD AL-MALIK

As the fifth Umayyad Caliph, Abd al-Malik reigned from 685 to 705. Whilst the Umayyads archnemesis, Ibn al-Zubayr had declared himself Caliph in Mecca, Abd al-Malik sought to stabilize the situation at home in Syria. One of his first actions was to negotiate peace with the Byzantines in 689, even though this made him very unpopular among his people. Like many Arab leaders, political rivalry and assassination plots were part of the game. Abd al-Malik took steps to protect himself, including countering a local coup d'état. Then he moved his attention to Iraq where he defeated the current governor, Mus'ab ibn al-Zubayr—installed as the region's leader by his brother Ibn al-Zubayr. The Battle of Maskin (near Baghdad) was a momentous victory for Abd al-Malik, as it made Ibn al-Zubayr's position even weaker without the aid of Iraq.

Then, Abd al-Malik turned his attention to Mecca. He sent his general to assassinate Ibn al-Zubayr which was carried out in 692. Once Ibn al-Zubayr was overthrown, Abd al-Malik consolidated Iran and Iraq with the Caliphate.

Abd al-Malik also paid much attention to cultural aspects of the empire. It was during his rule that significant monuments such as Dome of the Rock and holy mosques, Al-Aqsa Mosque and Haram al-Sharif, were built in Jerusalem.

Before he came to power, the empire was built on numerous nations of conquered tribes and bands of people. There had not been one language, but several, such as Greek, Persian, and other native languages. As a means of unifying the nation, Abd al-Malik introduced Arabic as an official and bureaucratic language. Finally, this Caliph also took an interest in developing the infrastructure of the empire, undertaking projects to construct dams, roads, and canals. Like many other caliphs before him, Abd al-Malik's death was the result of an illness, probably one of the plagues. He is remembered as being one of the greatest Umayyad leaders who brought peace and prosperity to the empire.

AL-WALID I

After his father's death, Al-Walid I was not destined to be the next caliph. It was the death of Abd al-Aziz ibn Marwan that allowed for Al-Walid I to become the next Umayyad leader.

The Islamic empire reached its peak in terms of prosperity and territory during Al-Walid I's reign. Al-Walid I, like his father, continued to undertake construction projects. For example, the historical Umayyad Mosque of Damascus, the Al-Asqa Mosque in Jerusalem, and the Prophet's Mosque in Medina were great works commissioned by Al-Walid. The last of these projects was an attempt to reconcile with the Medinese (people from Medina). Building such a stately mosque was a way of attaching historical importance to the city.

Unlike his father, he broke the truce with the Byzantines. The 19th-century historian, Julius Wellhausen, explains that Al-Walid reinvigorated the Caliphates armies by introducing fresh campaigns aimed at territorial expansion. He also turned his attention to central Asia and Iberia. It was when the Umayyad Caliphate entered Southern Iberia that the Umayyad Caliphate established itself more fully in Europe. In Transoxiana (now Kazakhstan, Uzbekistan, Tajikistan, and Kyrgyzstan), Al-Walid established settlements but preferred the diplomatic route, setting up alliances with the indigenous groups from whom the empire received tributes. A clear sign of the prosperity of the Caliphate was the introduction of social welfare programs. Using the empire's taxation program, Al-Walid I's primary focus was to aid the poor and disabled.

HISHAM IBN ABD AL-MALIK

Illness took Al-Walid I like many other caliphs. After a period of political instability from 715 to 724, Hisham took over. Rebellion seemingly appeared in every corner of the empire. The first of these was in Sindh (now Pakistan), where a group of Hindu dissidents carried out a revolt. Hisham's forces quashed the rebellion, reasserting Umayyad rule over the Indian subcontinent.

Towards the end of his reign, Hisham faced insurrection in North Africa in 740. There was a Berber revolt in response to Kharijite teachings. This group, the Kharijites, had long been a thorn in the Umayyad Caliphate's side. One of their main points of dispute was hereditary succession implemented by Muawiya I. In 740, they had enough power to dispel a force of 27,000 Syrian soldiers, sent by Hisham to put down their rebellion. Kairouan (in modern-day Tunisia) was besieged to break up the revolt. The Umayyads maintained their rule over North African Berbers, breaking up the Berbers and causing them to flee disunited from their clansmen. Yet, the death toll had been great.

There was another revolt in Iraq, where Zayd ibn Ali—a pro-Ali supporter who founded his own Shia sect—staged the insurrection. It was not only insurrection, but betrayal too as the Kufans, loyal to the Umayyad, encouraged Zayd ibn Ali to make a vie for power. It was also a clandestine affair, as Zayd ibn Ali tried to win the loyalty of the citizens of Kufah. The governor of Iraq responded quickly to the threat. A plan was set to search the city for Zayd ibn Ali, which ended with his death—his head sent to Hisham.

Naturally, these were brutal times, but Hisham continued with the work Al-Walid I had begun, such as the building of mosques and territorial expansion. Under Hisham, the Umayyads went even further into Europe, this time into France. Bordeaux was captured. Loire was next in line. What ensued was the Battle of Tours—one of the most memorable events in history. The French met the Umayyads in battle, and it resulted in a French victory. It also put a close on the Caliphate's further attempts to invade the continent.

The End of the Umayyad Caliphate

During Hisham's reign, the numerous rebellions were a sign of things to come. Once the Kharijite revolt was brought under control, change was stirring in Khurasan, a vast Persian plateau. Though Khurusan was governed by someone appointed by the Umayyad Caliph, the influence of Islam and Arab culture did not spread throughout the population. In Khurasan, there was much more mixture between the various ethnicities. While we have not touched on it yet, the rebellions that the Umayyad Caliphate suffered during its 89 years was often a response to the rigid social system that the Caliphate had set up. The Umayyad Caliphate was divided into four social classes: Muslim Arabs at the highest tier, non-Arab Muslims, non-Muslims, and slaves.

This inspired much discontent among the other non-Arab ethnicities such as the Persians, Berbers, and Egyptians, among others. Even though they had converted to Islam, they were still not wholly integrated into the society. As you have read, the Caliphate had conquered various peoples; the empire itself was made up of a larger non-Arab population than Arab. The lands conquered also had adherents of different faiths. While they were allowed to practice their religious rituals, they had to pay taxes, known as *jizyah*. The tax was unfair; its conditions were bred on an inequality predicated on religion. This is clearly stated in the following statement: "In return for payment of the jizyah, non-Muslim populations—specifically Jews and Christians—were granted protection of life and property and the right to practice their religion" (Afsaruddin, A. 2019). Paying taxes to guarantee protection of one's life did not breed friendship between Muslims and non-Muslims.

Additionally, the Umayyad Caliphate had taken over Persian territories. We have already read that Arabic was adopted as the official language, but this only aggravated the Persians, who preferred their tongue. Writing in Persian or Khwārezmian carried the death penalty. It was not only those who dared to write in a language other than Arabic who faced persecution, but Zoroastrians too.

Zoroastrianism was an Iranian religion that is said to be the ancestor of the Abrahamic religions like Islam. Only the Muslims under the Umayyad Caliphate did not consider such matters. Zoroastrian religious texts and holy buildings were destroyed. Since Iranians were non-Arabs, they were not appointed as governors in their own territories, but were instead assigned Umayyad governors. Persians who for centuries had great empires—and in recent memory—were proud people. Naturally, the steps the Umayyad had taken to erase their language and treat them as second-class citizens in their own land did not sit well with the Iranians. And then, there was dissent within the Arabs and Muslims themselves who did not believe in the hereditary tradition of the Caliphate, or that the original *Rashidun* had the right to rule after the death of Prophet Muhammed.

Historically speaking, there are few sources on the exact causes of the rebellion, but it has been agreed upon that it was general discontent which brought it about. It was particularly the Abbasid, Alawi, and Fatimid who were all vying for power. It was the Abbasid family who won the support of many citizens, orchestrating a revolt. Marwan II, caliph at the time, met the Abbasid forces at the Battle of the Zab, which ended in a defeat for Marwan II. After capturing Damascus in

April 750, the Abbasid Caliphate supplanted the Umayyads. They also made sure that the dynasty's bloodlines ended, taking brutal measures to kill all the remaining Umayyad family members. Abd ar-Rahman I escaped the massacre, fleeing to Córdoba in Spain and establishing the Emirate of Córdoba. While the Umayyad Caliphate had fallen, the Abbasid Caliphate had resurrected in its ashes.

The Umayyad Caliphate fell eleven years before its centennial, making its longevity much shorter than the empires of the Huns and Lombards. Nonetheless, both the Umayyads and Rashidun Caliphates achieved what these two empires failed to: a lasting impression or imprint on the culture of those countries. With the exception of the Iberian Peninsula (Portugal and Spain), the majority of areas comprising the Caliphates such as Pakistan, the Levant, parts of Persia, and North Africa continue to adhere to the Islamic faith and the Arab culture is still maintained.

It is pointed out that it was this rapid expansion of Islam ultimately drove the empire's downfall. Rebellions were frequent. Dissent among its various peoples was commonplace. The Umayyad leaders had conquered peoples who came from long traditions who were not specifically Muslim nor Arab, but the Umayyad Caliphate often suppressed or undermined the traditions and religions of those they had conquered. That being said, the Emirate of Córdoba survived to the 10th century, and Córdoba boomed under the Caliphate's rule.

CHAPTER FIVE

THE MOST SERENE REPUBLIC OF VENICE

c. 697–1797 CE

I t is ironic that one of the longest surviving medieval empires during the Middle Ages was literally built on shaky ground. Where land meets water in northeast Italy, a new empire was born—on water. No land means no resources, yet a powerful and prosperous empire was created—surviving 1100 years, taking Venice right from the end of the Roman Empire to the Age of Enlightenment.

In this chapter, we will explore *Serenissima Repubblica di Venezia*, more commonly known as *La Serenissima*, the Most Serene Republic of Venice, by first looking at its origins, conditions for imperial growth, and its eventual downfall.

Background

Once the Roman Empire disintegrated, Italy had fallen to the hands of various Germanic tribes. The population fled the interior to the coastal regions for safer ground—safer ground in this case meant not ground, but the lagoons of Venice. It was a good strategy as most nomadic groups occupied landlocked regions, meaning they lacked maritime skills.

Byzantium took control of Venice for a short time, putting it under the rule of the Exarchate of Ravenna, meaning it was a province of Byzantium. However, the people living in Venice were given the freedom to elect a leader over the lagoon. In 697, Paolo Lucio Anafesto was elected as Venice's first Doge.

The word 'doge' is unique to Venice as it was a special title existing only in this empire. The office of the Doge, established just before 700 CE, was the person who served as the civic, military and religious leader of Venice. The Doge was considered an honored servant, rather than a lord, of the people of Venice.

Anafesto's origins are not clear. Some historians state that he was from a noble family, while others, like the English historian John Julius Norwich, claim that he was the Exarch Paul—Leo III. Regardless of his true identity, Anafesto had some work to do. The Lombards were on their doorsteps; so were bands of Slavic tribes. If you are familiar with Venice's geography, you know it borders Slovenia, and across from the Adriatic Sea is its neighbor, Croatia. As the Doge's role was not limited simply to the commerce of Venice, Anafesto had to take steps to secure Venice from potential enemies.

In 727, Ursus Hypatus—also called Orso Ipato—was crowned the third Doge. With the election of Ursus Hypatus, we see a movement away from Byzantium. Anafesto was crowned Doge with the support of the Byzantines. On the other hand, Ursus was not backed by Byzantium. Like his predecessor, Ursus devoted much of his attention to preventing the Lombards from capturing Venice. During his 10-year reign, the Lombards invaded and captured Venice. Ursus Hypatus sent a force of 80 ships of trained archers and men-at-arms to take the lagoon back. It ended with a victory for the Venetians. Recapturing Ravenna also helped to separate Venice further from the Byzantine power, allowing the Byzantines to recognize their autonomy.

Ursus Hypatus' reign ended 10 years later, since war had broken out between Eraclea and Equilio (now Jesolo). Not only was it a violent civil war, but it caused the death of Ursus Hypatus. He sided with the Eracleans, agitating others who killed him. Ursus named his successor: his son Teodato Ipato, known also as Deusdedit. This attempt to hand down the title of Doge was Ursus' plan to create his own dynasty. As *La Serenissima* was a republic, this did not go down too well with the

Venetian occupants. Amidst this *La Serenissima* was going through a civil war.

The structure of the republic was that there was the *Maggior Consiglio*—the Great council—which was composed of 480 members from noble families. This means that the Doge's power was always limited. It also meant that when Deusdedit was ready to take over, he was instead sent into exile. For a brief period, the *Maggior Consiglio* reorganized the empire's structure so that the *magister militum* became the chief administrator. The *magister militum* was a kind of generalissimo, meaning he had the loyalty of the army. Nonetheless, the plan of the *Maggior Consiglio* was for the *magister militum* to be replaced every year. After the first *magister militum*, Felicius Cornicola came into the role. However, he recalled Deusdedit from exile. Returning from exile, Deusdedit was not appointed the new leader of Venice. It went to Giovanni Fabriciaco instead. Whether it was a plot on Deusdedit's part or not, insurrection occurred in the empire. Fabriciaco was to suffer Deusdedit's same fate years before: going into exile.

In 742, Deusdedit was officially crowned the vote through election. And for 13 years, he ruled the republic. One of his most notable moves as Doge was to move the capital from Eraclea to Malamocco (in Lido, one of the islands nearby). Unlike the two previous Doges, Deusdedit took steps to sign a peace treaty with the Lombards. Deusdedit's fortunes turned. Insurrection appeared once more in the kingdom.

Three blocs were competing for political dominance at the time. One was pro-Byzantine, the second pro-Frankish, and the last was pro-Lombard. Naturally, these groups could not find a political middle ground as some sought protection from the Lombards by moving closer to the Franks, while others believed peace with the Lombards would ensure greater prosperity in the Republic. The pro-Byzantine faction wished for neither. When Deusdedit arranged a peace treaty with the Lombards, anger was awakened. Ironically, though there were three factions competing for power, it also helped to bring political stability. It meant that governmental operations were consistently checked and scrutinized, preventing abuse of power or mismanagement.

Galla Gaulo became the fifth Doge, elected for taking down Deusdedit by blinding him and sending him into exile. A year later, Galla Gaulo met a similar fate after Domenico Monegario deposed him. With the support of the Lombards, Monegario became the sixth Doge. Wishing not to incur the anger of the pro-Frankish and pro-Byzantine factions, Monegario set up tributes to maintain peace with the Republic's rivals. It was also under this Doge that maritime developed dramatically, making Venice a pivotal leader in maritime and trade.

The Reign of the Participazio Doges

When the Carolingian Empire began its own expansion, it brought it precariously close to Byzantine territory. Naturally, this did not bode too well with the Byzantines. Sitting equally badly with Byzantium, Pope Leo III crowned Charlemagne as *Imperator Romanorum*, Emperor of the Romans. Already the Byzantines had a long-standing feud with the Papacy. The friction caused by such actions prevented negotiations over territory during 803, but a peace treaty called Pax Nicephori was signed, allowing the Franks and Byzantines to determine the extent of their empires. The fate of Venice was decided during the Pax Nicephori. Venice was declared to be under the sphere of Byzantine influence. The Byzantines, under ruler Nikephoros I, took this information literally.

In 807, the Byzantine fleet sailed to the republic and orchestrated the deposition of the current doge, Oblerius, installing a Byzantine governor in his place. Agnello Participazio was elected as the new doge. Agnello took steps to develop Venice's infrastructure, such as building bridges, canals, and fortifying the territory against possible attacks. Anticipating an attack from within the Republic, he built the Doge's palace which is still located by Saint Mark's square. The image of Venice that comes to mind now took its appearance and structure from Agnello's work. For example, Rivoalto (Rialto), the group of islands making up the current city, was developed to create the city center.

Saint Mark and the Patriarch of Venice

During the 9th century, Venice was trying to establish itself as a trading partner. Giustiniano Participazio, Agnello's son, contrived a plan to bring this about.

During this period, Christians made the pilgrimage to Egypt to visit the grave of Saint Mark. Giustiniano organized merchants to sail to Alexandria and secretly steal the saint's body. Hidden among pork, the merchants managed to sneak Saint Mark's body through customs and into Venice. The current Bishop (patriarch) of Venice accepted the body of Saint Mark. Soon constructions began to build St Mark's Basilica, a cathedral fitting for the holy figure. As a result, Venice developed its reputation among other nations and empires and its trading partners increased.

The body of Saint Mark had further consequences for the Republic. According to tradition, Mark was under Saint Peter's instructions to oversee the territory of Aquileia as Bishop. Once the body of Saint Mark was acquired, the jurisdiction of Aquileia (a city in Friuli-Venezia Giulia close to the Slovenia border) was to return to the bishop. Now Venice had a legitimate claim to Aquileia, establishing the Patriarchate of Aquileia.

A Patriarch has much power in the Catholic tradition. He is the highest-ranking Bishop, giving him extensive jurisdiction—in this case, Aquileia, Friuli, Treviso, Padua, and Trieste, now in northeast Italy—allowing the Republic to encroach on Byzantine territory.

Imperial Expansion and Prosperity in *La Serenissima*

Trade was integral to the economy of Venice. To make this possible they needed to secure the Adriatic Sea. Up to 1000 CE, the Participazio engaged in many wars with the Saracens and Slavs to establish themselves further. There were many battles that took place, including one in 887 which saw the death of Pietro I Candiano, the sixteenth Doge—the only one to die in battle as of then.

It was his son Pietro II Candiano, the nineteenth Doge, who eventually established Venetian dominance in the Adriatic Sea. Byzantium was weakening. Moreover, Pietro II Candiano annexed Istria—the protruding piece of land now shared by Croatia, Slovenia, and Italy—and Capodistria (a city in modern-day Slovenia).

Both Pietro II Candiano's son and his grandson would continue his ambitions expanding the Venetian empire. By the 11th century, Venice had organized treaties which involved paying tribute to the Dalmatians so merchants could have passage on the Adriatic Sea. Soon, they became a major power in this region. There were a number of reasons for this.

CAPITALIST/ANTI-FEUDAL STRUCTURE

Feudalism was the traditional structure in most of Europe. Mark Cartwright provides a definition of feudalism.

> Feudalism was the system in 10th–13th century European medieval societies where a social hierarchy was established based on local administrative control and the distribution of land into units (fiefs). A landowner (lord) gave a fief, along with a promise of military and legal protection, in return for a payment of some kind from the person who received it (vassal) (Cartwright, M. 2018).

You have already read in the introduction and first chapter that Europe did not enter some kind of period of darkness, but rather that industry and commerce exploded. A lot of development that took place in Europe was based on agriculture. The agricultural revolution was pivotal to Europe's success, but it was also fundamental to feudalism. Why, you ask? Because of land.

From Cartwright's definition, you see that land was fundamental for a landowner or ruler's control. Ultimately, it was the nobility, loyal to the king, who owned the lands. Farmhands and peasants toiled on these lands for payment.

What is unique about Venice was that it had no land or very little. Even today, there is almost no agricultural and mining activity in the region. The following quote indicates that under such conditions, feudalism was impossible in Venice: "With no lands, knights or serfs, the Venetian people had a mostly egalitarian society which, at the time, was certainly unique" (LDC, n.d.).

Commerce, trade, and mercantilism thrived instead, simply because the Venetians had no choice. Trade or starve. This is also pointed out by the next statement: "The difficulty of life in the lagoon bounded all of its inhabitants with solidarity and self-discipline. Venice lived between two worlds: the land and the sea, the East and the West" (LDC, n.d.).

It was the Republic's ability to adapt to mercantilism and become significant players in maritime trade that allowed them to prosper. As long as something could be traded, the Venetians had a market for it. With its anti-feudalist structure and its emphasis on trade, *La Serenissima* is recognized for being a major player in inspiring capitalism. Some even go so far as to say that Venice is the birthplace of modern capitalism.

Banking

With booming trade and commerce in Venice, it paved the way for the creation of the modern banking system. As Venice is situated on Italy's northeast coastline, it positioned the Republic to easily trade with the East. This includes trade with the Arabs in the Near East, which brought them in contact with Arabic numerals. Soon, *La Serenissima* adopted them, completely revolutionizing finance and accounting.

Prior to that the Republic had been using Roman numerals, which are still currently used in the rest of the peninsula. You can only imagine the impact of using Arabic numerals. Even today, the 1-to-10 digit system presently in use is based on the Arabic numerals, which takes its origins from Hindu numerals. The impact of using these Arabic-Hindu numeral systems is revealed.

They originated in India in the 6th or 7th century and were introduced to Europe through the writings of

Middle Eastern mathematicians, especially al-Khwarizmi and al-Kindi, about the 12th century. They represented a profound break with previous methods of counting, such as the abacus, and paved the way for the development of algebra (The Editors of Britannica., 2022).

Mathematical calculations became much easier to perform with the transition to Arabic-Hindu numerals. As Venetian commerce was based on trade, many seafarers found it difficult to carry around all their earnings from abroad, so the banking system was created.

Slave Trade

Unfortunately, like many others, Venice also profited from a darker industry: slavery. In the 15th century, Venice sold slaves to the Moors in North Africa. At first, they bought slaves in Italy. According to an article on labor, "In Venice between 1414 and 1423 alone, at least 10,000 such slaves changed hands" (Rawlins, G.J.E., 2008). However, in about 840 in accordance with the Pactum Lotharii, the selling of Christian slaves to Muslim owners became outlawed. So, the Venetians turned their attention to non-Christians—namely, the Slavs.

On the northeast border, numerous Slavic peoples regularly attacked the Italian peninsula; as the Venetian empire expanded, *La Serenissima* moved further into Slavic territories including modern-day Slovenia, Montenegro, and Croatia. Venice, with its established trade network with the Moors, thrived as a result of the slave trade during this period.

Religious Tolerance

Much of Europe had become engaged in the Crusades from 1095 to 1291. The Venetians knew that disrupting their trade would impact their economy, so they continued trade, exhibiting religious tolerance despite the Crusades occurring at the time. The republic got involved in the fourth Crusade, but once again their involvement was instigated by profit rather than religious calling.

Political Structure

With the presence of so many competing factions, this could have led to the empire's downfall. However, the Venetians realized this and could transform this into one of their strengths. The competition among the factions meant that power was divided and there was the employment of many councilors and officials to perform checks so that there were no issues with mismanagement or abuse of power. Even if there was so much division among the civilians of Venice, there was stability, allowing the empire to thrive in commerce and trade. As we have already seen in the chapter on the Lombards and Umayyads, political stability was rare.

Additionally, the Venetian political structure continuously evolved. From 742 to 1032 (known as the Ducal period), the Doge held absolute power. It is true that there were four institutions who assisted him with administration. They were the *Consilium Sapientes*, *Curia*, *Ducal Gastaldi*, and *Concio*. The *Consilium Sapientes* was also known as the Minor Council or Ducal Council, acting as the personal board of the Doge and meaning they had some influence over the legislation. The *Ducal Gastaldi* were civil and military officials while the *Curia* had power over the judiciary. However, the *Curia* was controlled by the Doge. Furthermore, if one of the *Ducal Gastaldi* failed to perform his duties, the Doge could take his title and office away. Thus, during the Ducal Period, the Doge exerted much control over the empire.

In 1032, the Communal Period began which saw the evolution of the *Consilium Sapientes* into four institutions: *Maggior Consiglio*, *Quarantia*, *Minor Consiglio*, and *Consiglio dei Pregadi*. With the introduction of these four institutions, the power the Doge once had, diminished greatly, and evolved to simply a ceremonial one. The *Quarantia* took over many government and supreme court functions. And finally, the *Consiglio dei Pregadi* were responsible for sensitive and urgent matters in the empire.

The political organization of Venice evolved once more during 1296. During this period, only aristocrats could be elected to the various institutions and governmental roles, thus giving rise to the name of the period, the Aristocratic Period.

In order to distinguish who is an aristocrat, The Golden Book was introduced with the names of the aristocratic families. So the Concio, whose main function was to decide who could be a member of other institutions, was not needed anymore and it eventually was abolished in 1423 AD

In many ways, the political structure in Venice during its long existence, especially from the Communal Period onwards, reflects a similar governmental structure in many nations around the world. It still provides a voice or representation of minorities and results in an election of a popular figure, but also ensures that power is not concentrated into the hands of one central leader.

These are some of the main factors which contributed to the prosperity of the Venetian Republic. However, there were numerous other reasons which allowed the republic to expand. The Venetians engaged in slave trade like other nations at the time, simply because they traded in everything and with everyone. If something—meaning anything—could be sold, the Venetians traded it. Furthermore, they became masterclass traders because they were willing to do business with everyone, including trading with Levantine and Egyptian sultans during the Crusades.

13th Century

You have already seen that the Venetians acted kind of like mercenaries during the fourth Crusade. Well, the price for these mercenaries was Zara. Under Doge Enrico Dandolo, coming into power in 1192, the leaders of the fourth Crusade offered to pay the Venetians for transportation to the conflict—except they couldn't pay.

When they defaulted, Enrico Dandolo negotiated their assistance in the capture of Zara (a city in Croatia on the Dalmatian coast). The siege on the city was successful. Despite the Pope excommunicating the entire Crusade army for its involvement, the Venetians continued with their path of destruction undeterred. This time, their destination was Constantinople.

The sacking of Constantinople has gone down as one of the most disgraceful sieges, except that it was immensely profitable. The Byzantines had a long history, spanning 1000 years. Their culture was rich; so were their art pieces and scrolls. They had also collected numerous artifacts from Ancient Greece and Rome. When the Crusaders sacked the city, they either melted some of these artifacts for their commodity value or stole precious art such as the Horses of Saint Mark statue, changing name as it changed ownership. This stolen relic remains displayed inside Saint Mark's Basilica in Venice.

Almost a decade later, the Venetians became embroiled in another war. This time it was an internal conflict—the Paduans and Trevisani siding against the Venetians. At a festival in Treviso, the Venetians insulted both the Paduans and Trevisani. Conflict ensued. The Venetians did not fare so well this time. An attack on Venetian territory allowed the Paduans to capture 400 soldiers. The weather intervened, forcing the Paduans and reinforcements from Treviso to retreat. Fortunately, again for the Venetians, the Patriarch of Aquileia also intervened, negotiating peace treaties with the nations.

In the following decade, fear of the Mongol Empire had spread throughout Europe. As diplomatic and pragmatic as ever, the Venetians signed a trade treaty with the Mongols. It proved to be an intelligent move, as by the end of the century, the Venetians had to prepare themselves for a war with the Genovese.

THE WAR WITH GENOA

There were some similarities between Genoa and Venice. Both enjoyed much maritime power and both economies grew rapidly from trade. Like Venice, coastal towns such as Genoa were spared much of the onslaught which inland cities and towns were subjected to, allowing them to develop in relative stability.

Genoa's autonomy came much later. Only in the 11th century were they given sovereignty. While Venice had once been a state of the Byzantines, Genoa fell under the territory of the Carolingian (Frankish) empire, delaying their freedom by some centuries. Venice's trade route was the Adriatic Sea, East Italy. Genoa began to dominate the Tyrrhenian Sea, West Italy, giving both room and freedom to prosper. Yet, in the 13th century, the situation changed.

After the Fourth Crusade, Byzantine and Genoa formed an alliance, prompting Genoa to regain dominance in the Mediterranean since the Byzantines gave free trading rights to the Genoese. As trade was Venice's lifeline, they responded to Genoa's increasing power with conflict. In the last decade of the 13th century, Pietro Gradenigo—the 49th Doge—sent 68 ships to attack a Genoese port in Turkey. For almost the next century, the fighting continued. Four battles were fought. At first Genoa got the upper hand, but in 1380 the Venetians defeated the Genoese, maintaining their mercantile dominance.

14th Century

Venetian imperial expansion continued as it annexed the cities of Mestre and Serravalle in 1337, Treviso and Bassano del Grappa in 1339, and later in the century, Oderzo in 1380 and Ceneda in 1389. Furthermore, imperial expansion also took on a colonist form as Venice created a colony in Candia (now Crete). There was an uprising in the island who wished for Candia's independence, but by 1368, Candia was under Venetian rule.

15th Century

The empire grew both within the Italian peninsula and outwards. Along the Dalmatian coast, Venice acquired territory from Istria to Albania. Such expansions were necessary as they provided safe passage along their trade routes in the Adriatic. Inland, they had managed to not only take over many of the cities in the modern Veneto region including Verona and Padua, but they also slowly encroached on territories in

Lombardy such as Brescia, Bergamo, and Cremona towards the end of the empire.

Decline

Venice continued in a healthy state beyond the medieval age, but it would eventually come to an end. The world was a different place after the French Revolution and Napoleon in power. Ideas such as democracy and royal or aristocratic rule were outdated, especially in France's eyes.

In 1796, the new leader of the French republic used Venice as a base for conducting military operations in Austria. Venice was neutral in those affairs between the Austrians and French, so they allowed the French occupation only to their own demise. Jacobin notions (strongly against a ruling aristocracy) covertly spread through *La Serenissima* and soon, internal conflict weakened the empire. Bergamo and Brescia broke away. On May 12th, 1796, the Doge Ludovico Manin abdicated and the *Maggior Consiglio* declared the end of the Most Serene Republic.

Many people speak with great concern about the sinking city of Venice. What many people overlook is the incredulity of the city's very existence. There are massive Baroque, Renaissance, and much earlier marble buildings supported by only wooden poles and platforms.

The Venetians had little choice but to flee to safe ground—in this case, not ground at all. Against all odds, they became a massive maritime power and built a sprawling empire. They dominated the Adriatic Sea and much of the Mediterranean Sea. How they accomplished this feat without land or agriculture confounds historians, but one thing is for sure—they played to their strengths.

They used their divided empire to create a political structure where power was not concentrated. Their lack of resources spurred them on to be leaders in trade and mercantilism. And they use the protection of water—a supermassive moat—to keep invaders out. The name the Most Serene Republic of Venice speaks of the tranquility and political stability that existed in few places in the Middle Ages.

CHAPTER SIX

THE FIRST BULGARIAN EMPIRE

c. 681–1018 CE

E astern European and Eurasian history share as much limelight as Western or West European counterparts. These regions have a long history, spanning often to prehistoric days. Even in the medieval period, these nations had fascinating empires like that of Bulgaria. Like with many events in the Middle Ages, the catalyst for the creation of this empire was the fall of Western Roman Empire. Yet, their history was to be shaped more by the Byzantine Empire and their settlement in Southeast Europe.

In this chapter, we will analyze the First Bulgarian Empire whose frontiers reached Byzantium, the Northeast Balkans, and the Black Sea. During this age, the first Bulgarian Empire emerged as the cultural and spiritual capital of Slavic Europe. We will also consider how this empire gave rise to Bulgarian identity, one that is maintained to the modern day and is integral to contemporary Bulgaria.

Origins of the Bulgars

During the 5th century, the Bulgars were based by the Kerch Strait, where the Huns had settled before their conquest west. When the Hunnic Empire collapsed, the Huns returned to the Kerch Strait, where they were absorbed into the Bulgars.

There is some debate among historians about the exact origins of the Bulgars. There is speculation that they are a Turkic group. Other Turkic groups in modern times live in Turkey, Azerbaijan, and the other Eurasian '-stan' states. This means the Bulgars would be from a Eurasian or Central Asian background.

The proto-Turkic word 'bulgar' could mean either "to stir" or "to mix." Using these linguistic clues, 'stir' implies that they were troublemakers, rebels, or colloquially, stirrers. On the contrary, "to mix" denotes a mixed group of people whose bloodlines have been crossed. There was some discussion as to whether it was their mixing bloodlines with the Huns that gave rise to the term 'Bulgar.' However, as historians point out it would be impossible for an ethnic group to have emerged over such a short time. Following this train of thought, the homeland of the 'Bulgars' is said to be Kazakhstan or the Northern Caucasus region.

Another train of thought posits them as a group native to the west side of the European Steppe, approximately in Ukraine and the European part of Russia. In this case, their ancestry would be more closely related to Western Europeans. Finally, there is one group of thinking that believes they were once a group of Scythians, who were originally Iranians (Karatay, O., 2003).

First Contact With Rome

Unlike the Huns, who arrived on the European scene to torment the Byzantines, the initial relationship with the Bulgars was different. In 480, the Bulgars were hired by the Byzantines to fight against the Ostrogoths who had been tormenting the Roman Empires then. Using the Bulgars to help get rid of the Ostrogoth menace seemed an excellent strategy, except that paying these mercenaries had given them a taste for gold.

Beginnings of the Empire

There had been some back and forth with the Bulgars. It is believed that when the Huns moved into Europe, the Bulgars had gone with them. Later, when they fled, the Bulgars joined the Huns once more. In 632, Kubrat Khan had become the ruler of this band of people. In what is called the "Old Great Bulgaria" (now Crimea), the Bulgars thrived.

Kubrat made his five sons promise that they would never separate and remain in the region, believing there was strength in numbers. On his death, there was internal conflict threatening political stability. Also, the security of "Old Great Bulgaria" was now in jeopardy, as a semi-nomadic group called the Khazars attacked the band in 668. This attack on the Bulgars sparked the breakdown of the Bulgars into smaller tribes. Kubrat's sons soon parted ways.

Asparukh (also Asparuh) took approximately 30,000 to 50,000 Bulgars into Europe. Michael the Syrian, patriarch of the Syrian Orthodox Church, writing in the 12th century suggests that the population who traveled with Asparukh only numbered 10,000.

First, they migrated to Bessarabia (Moldova) and in the next decade, they crossed the Danube into Scythia Minor (composed of modern-day Romanian and Bulgarian parts). As they were first aligned with the Eastern Romans, they were given the go-ahead to settle in the Balkans region, north of Byzantium. At the time, Byzantium had its hands full with constant invasions by the Umayyad Caliphate in the south. They reluctantly relinquished the Danube region. Yet, under Justinian I, they vowed to get it back.

Though Byzantium fortified the Danube region, in 680 they led an attack under Constantine IV against the Bulgars, who had now become their northern threat. The Byzantines organized a huge military effort against their northern neighbors in a hope to reclaim the land. This was to be the Byzantines' second significant loss. Weakened by the previous conflict with the Umayyad Caliphate, the Byzantines could not repel the Bulgars. Their loss resulted in their signing a costly peace treaty with the Bulgars. The terms of the treaty were that Byzantine recognized the Bulgars as an independent state. And so, the Bulgar Empire was born.

Its capital was put in place in Pliska (now in Northern Bulgaria). Another term stipulated that an annual tribute be paid and territories handed over to the Bulgars.

The Bulgars could not withstand an attack from the Byzantines on their own. On entering the Balkans and Danube Region, the Bulgars encountered various Slavic clans. It is unclear what kind of relationship existed between the Bulgarians and Seven Slavic Tribes. The Bulgarian historian, Vasil Zlatarski, describes their relationship as one of mutual agreement. However, numerous other historians suggest that the Bulgarians had in fact subjugated them. Once victory against the Byzantines was achieved, safeguarding various territories within the newfound kingdom was delegated to the Seven Clans. For example, the Severi clan was relocated to the Eastern Mountain passes to guard them from the Byzantines.

Early 8th Century

The Khazars remained the Bulgars' menace. In 700, the king Asparukh was killed in battle against them. His son Khan Tervel was his successor. The reign of Tervel is most known for his alliance with the Byzantines, or more specifically, with Justinian II. After being deposed, Justinian II approached Tervel for support to get him reinstated as emperor of Byzantium. In exchange for an army of 15,000 provided by Tervel, Justinian II gave the Bulgarian king gifts, his daughter's hand in marriage, and an alliance. Justinian II and Tervel were successful, allowing Justinian to execute his deposers. For his aid, Tervel was crowned kaisar (Caesar)—becoming the only foreign king to receive such a title and making him inferior to only the Byzantine emperor—and territory was ceded to the Bulgarians in northeast Thrace.

Friendship with the Byzantines did not last long. Three years later, Justinian II tried to recover the lost territory. In 708, at the Battle of Anchialus (in modern-day Bulgaria) the Byzantines reached the fortress of Anchialus where they set up camp, only to fall victim to a surprise attack from the Bulgarians. Justinian II managed to escape the scene, but many of the Byzantines were killed or taken as hostages.

A revolution in Asia Minor (Turkey) meant that Justinian II required yet again the help of the Bulgars in 711. This time Tervel was not so ready to come to his aid. The lack of friendship came with an underwhelming support of 3000 soldiers, resulting in the rebels gaining the upper hand and capturing Justinian II—who paid the price with his life. Six years later, Leo III the Isaurian was inaugurated emperor of Byzantium. And this time, it was the Byzantines who were on the receiving end of an invasion. The Umayyad Caliphate attempted to take the city of Constantinople by sea and land during 717 to 718. The new emperor, Leo III, appealed to Tervel, which Tervel agreed to. During the Second Siege of Constantinople, the Bulgars commenced an offensive on the rear of the Arabs; the Bulgars managed to kill approximately 22,000 Arabs, enough to drive the Arabs home.

Political Instability

While the Bulgars helped Byzantine leaders out of a few tight spots, for the remainder of the 8th century their relationship was marked with hostility. By the mid-century, the empire was riddled with instability mostly due to relations with Byzantines. Khan Sevar, from the Dulo clan ruling at the time, died after ruling from 738 to 753. For the rest of the century, the Bulgarian empire would be gravely impacted.

Over the next 15 years, seven leaders would take the reins of the empire only to be murdered. The main issue causing the turmoil among the Bulgars, according to Byzantine sources, was that there were two factions: one who wished for peace with the Byzantines and the other who wanted the opposite. To make matters worse, the original peace treaty signed between the two empires expired in 755. Though the Bulgars had come to Byzantium's aid against the Arabs, this didn't stop the Byzantines from launching attack after attack on the Bulgarians.

The first of these was the Battle of Marcellae in 756, ordered by Byzantine leader Constantine V. This would be the first of many victories against the Bulgarians. In Byzantine opinion, they were hoping to take advantage of the weakening Bulgarian empire owing to political divide to recover their lost territories. At the Battles of Anchialus and Berzitia in 763 and 774 respectively, the Byzantines defeated the Bulgars. Despite suffering many defeats and massive devastation, the Byzantines could not conquer them.

Some years after their disastrous military campaigns, the Bulgarians won a critical battle, after trapping the Byzantines in a mountain pass. This would become one of their trademark military strategies. Though the leader then won a crucial victory, he also aimed to make peace with the Byzantines. This did not go down well with the other Bulgar nobles, and he became one of the seven leaders murdered. The next Bulgar leader experienced a similar fate, not because he tried to make peace with the Byzantines but because he lost a battle, the second one at Anchialus.

Restoration of Order and Expansion

Before the end of the century, Khan Kardam became the ruler of the Bulgarian empire. Knowing it was only a matter of time before the Byzantines struck again, Kardam took an aggressive policy: attack to avoid being attacked. With this, the Bulgarians launched an attack and Kardam secured an important victory again at Marcellae in 792. After Kardam managed to bring peace among the bickering nobles in the empire, he immediately began to expand the empire's territory in what is today's Macedonia. Byzantium wasted no time in responding to this threat of Bulgarian expansion and launched a new attack in Marcellae, hoping to distract the Bulgarians from their ambitions in Macedonia. It was a huge mistake on the part of Constantine VI, as the Bulgarians defeated them. From the Bulgarian camp, things were looking more positive. Kardam restored order to the empire.

Going into the new century, the Bulgarian empire entered a new phase: one of stability and consolidation. Kardam's reign ended in 803 and Krum took the reins. Krum's first indication of his superior leadership came in 805, when he destroyed the Pannonian Avars and reclaimed territories in Ongal (now in Romania) (Fine, J.V.A.,1991).

KRUM

In 807, the Bulgarians launched attacks in the Struma valley (named after a river that flows into Greece and Bulgaria), defeating the Byzantine forces there. Two years later, the Bulgarians invaded the city Serdica (modern-day Sofia). 6000 were slaughtered at Serdica, arousing the wrath of Nikephoros I. The Byzantine ruler responded by attacking the Bulgarians, even invading their capital Pliska. The Bulgarians' capital city was sacked and destroyed. However, under Krum, they led a deadly and surprising counterattack when the Byzantines were returning to Constantinople. Not only was it one of the costliest defeats the Byzantines had suffered, but Nikephoros I was slain at the Battle of Pliska. Legend has it that Nikephoros I's skull was lined with silver and used as Krum's drinking cup.

The Bulgarian empire reached new heights with Krum. Their territory doubled during his 11 years in power. The empire then included the lands between the Danube and Moldova (now Romania) and under Krum they annexed Adrianople (now Edirne). The Bulgarians were getting closer to the capital Constantinople forcing the Byzantines to ask the Frankish for assistance. Fortunately for Byzantium, Krum died suddenly, ending the campaign for Constantinople.

KHAN OMURTAG

The historian Vasil Gyuzelev explains that after Krum's sudden death, there was a very short period of political instability in the empire. It is assumed that three nobles, who had also been Krum's generals, acted as regents to the throne. Omurtag took over when he came of age.

One of the first actions Omurtag took as ruler was to settle a 30-year peace treaty with the Byzantines. Given the history with Byzantium, it was not an easy decision to make but it proved to be a decisive one. There were a number of factors which brought Omurtag to negotiate peace with Byzantium. First, the Bulgarian empire had also grown in size. In the steppe regions of Eastern Europe, possible revolt was stirring among the tribes under Bulgarian control. Furthermore, the Frankish empire had also emerged and the Bulgarians were unclear how they would act. What Omurtag needed was time to consolidate the Bulgarian empire in the Steppes, which he bought with the 30 years of peace with the Byzantines.

Both empires recovered during this period. It was clearly advantageous to both, as in 820 when Michael II became the new Byzantine emperor, it was renewed. Once again, it was demonstrated to be necessary for the Bulgarians. A rebellious Byzantine military leader named Thomas the Slav orchestrated a siege in Constantinople, and Omurtag responded by aiding Michael II to put down the rebellion.

Moreover, Omurtag used this time to remove tribal leaders and replace them with his deputies, allowing for more centralized rule. Though Omurtag's attempts at diplomacy worked with the Byzantines, they failed with the Frankish empire. Omurtag tried to negotiate diplomacy between the two empires, but the Bulgarians had to resort to militaristic campaigns in 826 and 827 against the French to retain their strongholds in the Pannonia.

Omurtag also implemented a number of construction projects including building palaces and fortresses in the Danube region and restoring the capital, Pliska. The New Palace, also called the Palace of Omurtag in Shumen, and a temple were commissioned. Such lavish projects indicated that the Bulgarian empire had experienced a period of prosperity under Omurtag, thanks to the peace with the Byzantines.

Bulgarian Culture and Identity

Almost two decades after Omurtag, Boris I—son of Presian I and possibly great grandson of Omurtag—became ruler of the Bulgarian empire. His rule commenced in 852 and it began on a rocky note.

For a decade, the Bulgarians were engaged in military conflict with the Byzantines, the East Frankish Empire, Great Moravia, Serbs, and Croats. To add to Boris I's burdens, in August 863, an earthquake followed by lingering aftershocks impacted that year's harvest. Swarms of locusts then also attacked their crops. The consequence was that the Bulgarian empire was sent into famine. Despite these trying circumstances, under Boris I the empire did not incur much territorial loss.

RELIGION

In 864 Boris I was baptized in secret under the name Michael—taking his godfather's name who was Emperor Michael III—and introduced Christianity as a state religion, which was considered a "political move" (Halsey, E., 2020). So long as Bulgarians were pagans, they would be considered outsiders in Europe. By declaring Christianity as the state religion, it also brought the empire some prominence among other European Empires such as the Holy Roman and Byzantine Empires.

One problem appeared. Boris I was unclear on which branch of Christianity. By that time, Christianity had experienced a number of schisms; theological concepts and organization brought dissent. Though the East-West Schism or Great Schism took place two centuries later, during Boris I's reign a cultural divide, known as Greek East and Latin West, was already occurring in Western and Eastern Europe.

Eastern Orthodoxy was predominant in the Eastern half, while Western Christianity or Catholicism dominated the Western half. Boris I opted for Orthodoxy which brought him closer to the Byzantines, but with the creation of the Bulgarian Orthodox Church, it remained autocephalous, meaning that the Archbishop was a member of the Bulgarian Orthodox Church. In the case of Catholicism, even the high-ranking Bishop of the church would be under the Papacy's jurisdiction. Such a move also brought the Bulgarians closer to the Byzantines. Bulgarians now were welcomed into Byzantium where they could pursue a monastic education. When they returned to Bulgaria, they could join the ranks of the Orthodox Church, replacing previously Byzantine church leaders with those originally from within the Bulgarian empire.

Introducing Christianity as a state religion also brought about internal stability. The temple Omurtag had commissioned to be built was a Tengri one. Tengri was a Turkic pagan religion that was brought into Europe by the Bulgars and Huns. While it adhered to belief in a supreme being—making it somewhat monotheistic—it did recognize the existence of lesser gods. While Tengri was the religion of the Bulgar nobility, the other tribes making up the empire ascribed to a more polytheistic religion, creating a division among the peoples of the empire. By introducing a state religion that was neither Pagan nor Tengri, Boris I unified the peoples of the Bulgarian empire.

NATIONAL IDENTITY

Differences in religious belief created a divide among the peoples of the empire. It was not only varying religious practices, but for a long time, the empire had been plagued by cultural differences. The Bulgars made up the higher rungs of society ruling over peoples from various tribal bands. While we did not cover it earlier, one of Krum's critical changes was to introduce a legal code into the empire, protecting even those from poorer classes. The other laws may have been stricter such as prohibiting drinking and robbery, which carried harsh punishments, giving Krum a reputation of being a fair and just ruler.

With the conversion to Christianity, it was easier to craft a national identity as the religious plurality would be removed. Later in 886, the governor of Belgrade—acting under Boris I's instruction—welcomed the Saints Cyril and Methodius from Great Moravia (now composed of various Eastern European nations, mostly Czech Republic).

Owing to this cultural and religious divide in Europe between Orthodoxy and Western Christianity, these saints were expelled from Great Moravia. Disciples of Saints Cyril and Methodius also entered the empire. They adapted the writings and teachings of these Saints into a Cyrillic language, forming the basis of many Eastern European and Slavic languages. Now, the teachings of the Saints as well as the language helped to unify the various peoples of this nation, allowing the empire to have the foundations to create a nation-state. It is the reason why there is a country or nation called Bulgaria in the present-day, but for other bands of people such as the Avars and Khazars none such exist.

MILITARY

The Bulgars have many similarities with the Huns. They were also formidable warriors, especially so with cavalry. It is little wonder why the Byzantines initially sought their help against the Ostrogoths.

As we have already seen, division among the conquered peoples of the Danube caused political instability and prevented the Bulgarians from fostering a national identity. This division was further exacerbated within the military forces. The noble Bulgars were formidable horsemen. The peoples they conquered often made-up ranks of Slavic infantry. It was only under Omurtag that the army was unified so that there was not such a strict division between these two regiments.

The Golden Age

Spiridon Palauzov, a nineteenth-century Russian-Bulgarian historian, called the age of Simeon I the Great's reign "The Golden Age" or "Golden Age of Bulgaria." The capital was moved to Preslav (modern-day Shumen) under the new leader's instruction.

Simeon I's rule commenced with Byzantium closing off its market and trade with the Bulgarians. Knowing this would affect the empire's prosperity, Simeon I declared war on Byzantium. Owing to the might of the empire, the Byzantines could often rely on alliances and gold to pay for mercenaries to help them in times of conflict. When Simeon I made his announcement, the Byzantines turned to the Magyars, a band of people from the Ural Mountains and Volga region later called the national-ethnic group, Hungarians. At first, the Magyars defeated the Bulgarians, but the Bulgarians formed an alliance of their own with Pechenegs—semi-Nomadic Turkic peoples living on the borders of Byzantium. With the Pechenegs, the Bulgarians won. The Magyars were crushed and forced to return to Pannonia, where the kingdom of Hungary was to be founded.

A year later in 896, Simeon I got vengeance. At the Battle of Boulgarophygon, the Bulgarians met the Byzantines. It was a catastrophic loss for the Byzantines. Simeon I used the weakening Byzantine—who had lost their military general—and this defeat to his advantage. The Bulgarians then marched for Constantinople. On their path, they razed every village to the ground, clearly sending a message to the Byzantines. The emperor, Leo VI, got the message. He resorted to using Arab prisoners to try to repel the Bulgarians, but was eventually forced to sign a peace treaty. Naturally, the terms were advantageous to the Bulgarians: Byzantine markets were reopened to the Bulgarians, the entire Balkans region was established as Bulgarian land, annual tribute was to be paid once more to the Bulgarians, and they were to be deemed a favorable nation.

Even though both empires had signed a peace treaty, the Bulgarians continued to be a menace to the Byzantines, attacking various territories. Though Alexander Porphyrogenitus had a brief year-long rule over Byzantium, he decided to stop paying the Bulgarians their annual tribute. At that time, Simeon I was looking for any reason that justified war. And Alexander Porphyrogenitus gave it to him when he ended the tribute. Simeon I's ambitions were to invade Constantinople. With Constantinople conquered, a new Roman-Bulgarian empire could be formed, and Simeon I would be recognized as Emperor or Tsar. The Battle of Achelous saw the Bulgarian forces meet those of Byzantium, where they clashed at the Achelous River in south-eastern Bulgaria. Considered as the one of the worst battles of the medieval age or the "Battle of the Century," the Battle of Achelous was one of the Bulgarians' most successful military campaigns, but at the expense of the Byzantines. Tens of thousands of Roman soldiers died.

Such a victory made the Bulgarians equal to the Byzantines. The former's imperial prestige was acknowledged. Their rule in the Balkans was firmly established. Not only had the war cost much life for both groups but it had also been expensive to both, ushering in a much-needed period of recovery. For forty years, the Byzantines and Bulgarians enjoyed peace, allowing the Bulgarian empire to prosper once more.

Ironically, it was the newfound heights that the Bulgarian empire reached with Simeon I that ultimately brought about its downfall. It now became a target surrounded by many aggressive neighbors including the Magyars in the northwest, the Pechenegs, Kievan Rus in the northeast, and the Byzantines to their south. For though peace existed between the Byzantines and Bulgarians, it could never be fully guaranteed. In 968, the Kievan Rus invaded the empire and captured the capital in Preslav. Fortunately, the Bulgarians could regroup and recover in their territories in the south. However, by the end of the century, relations between the Byzantines had soured. For 40 years they fought. The Magyars participated as allies to the Byzantines. As resilient and relentless as the Bulgarians proved themselves to be, a critical loss in the Battle of Kleidion (southwest Bulgaria) brought about the Bulgarian empire's downfall. For the next four years, the Bulgarians continued to resist and defend, but for the next century and a half, the empire was swallowed up by the Byzantines.

It took about 130 years for the Bulgarians to build their empire to contend with the others present in Europe at that time. It took almost that amount of time for it to disintegrate. Nonetheless, the Bulgars had achieved what many bands and tribes had failed to do. They created an empire which received imperial recognition in Europe. And they established the foundations of a national identity—the Bulgarian one.

CHAPTER SEVEN

THE VIKINGS

c. 793–1066 CE

It is almost impossible to believe that the Vikings (also Norsemen or Northmen) rowed across the Atlantic to North America simply on their longboats. It was not Christopher Columbus but Leif Erikson, or "Leif the Lucky," a Norseman, who was the first European to set foot in the New World.

The Viking discovery of America is one of the more recently discovered facts. In the late 8th century, the Vikings—a class of seafaring warriors—took to the seas, left their base in Scandinavia, and for almost three centuries they tormented coastal villages, the British Isles, and parts of the European continent. Known for their violent raids and piracy, the Vikings left their mark on the Middle Ages. In this section, we will cover the Viking Age describing the origins, rise, and decline of these bands of people.

Origins of the Vikings

One of the main misconceptions of the Vikings is that the term 'Viking' was used for a race of people. People tend to believe they originate from Scandinavia, but peoples from Finland, Estonia, and Saami (parts of northern Sweden, Denmark, and Russia) also made up their ranks (History.com Editors., 2019). Rather, the term 'Viking' refers to a class of people. In fact, the word 'Viking' was derived from the Scandinavian root 'vik' meaning 'bay' or 'creek,' eventually giving rise to the Scandinavian term '*vikingr*' translating to 'pirate' or "a person who raids bays and creeks" (1).

Not all Scandinavians were Vikings. The editors of History.com provide more insight on this class of people. It was not only their "line of business" (i.e raiding and pillaging) that united them, but they were also considered uncivilized and not Christian. Typically, the Vikings constituted various landowning chiefs or clan hands who exercised rule over the clan. As they were landowners, they most likely were farmers, but when they left their homebase they took up a life of plundering and pillaging.

The exact reasons why they left Scandinavia are unknown. Some suggestions proposed overpopulation of the region. In this case, we can gain much knowledge about their reasons by analyzing their behavior. It seems unlikely that overpopulation provoked their travels south. They were pillages, raiders, and plunders. They left their homebase in search of wealth, not land. You can also rely on what you have learned up to now about the Middle Ages. As opposed to Europe being thrown into a period of darkness, the continent was becoming increasingly wealthier. It was these riches which drew the Norsemen south.

As maritime and seafaring developed in Europe, but especially in the British Isles, the Vikings (pirates) became attracted to the wealth in these regions. For their part, the Scandinavians also contributed their own commodities to the market, namely furs which were valued highly in European trade. It was this trade with the Scandinavians which probably brought the Scandinavians into contact with European and British trade and ports, which became sitting ducks—vulnerable to attack from foreign plunderers.

Early Raids

The Viking Age is said to have commenced in June 793 when the Vikings attacked Lindisfarne, a monastery on an island close to Northumberland (an English county bordering Scotland). In fact, this was not the first raid in the continent. Three years earlier, three Viking boats landed in Wessex and had initiated an attack there. However, this raid in Lindisfarne was more significant in nature. Joanna Story explains why this is the case.

> [T]he assault on Lindisfarne was different because it attacked the sacred heart of the Northumbrian kingdom, desecrating 'the very place where the Christian religion began in our nation.' It was where Cuthbert (d. 687) had been bishop, and where his body was now revered as that of a saint (Story, J., n.d.).

News of the Viking desecration had soon reached pious scholars and leaders in the continent. Naturally, the continent was disturbed by the attack. History.com editors reveal, "the attack shook the European religious world to its core" (History.com Editors., 2019). While they contemplated why such an atrocity had been allowed to happen, the Vikings, unperturbed, continued with their raids.

In 795, monasteries on the Hebridean Islands Skye and Iona and Rathlin (an island of Northern Ireland) were the next targets of Viking pillages. Before the end of the century, the British Isles had been hotspots for Viking raids. And just before the turn of the century, Viking radius of attack increased; St. Philibert's monastery in Noirmoutier-en-l'Île (Northeast France) was attacked in 799.

While the Viking attacks were increasing in frequency and expanding in their range, they were characteristically hit-and-run raids. These warriors were not seeking to expand their territories and extend Viking territory. Typically, they were also confined to coastal areas in the British Isles. One such trading center, Dorestad, was plundered frequently after 830. The British Isles were especially vulnerable to the Vikings because towns were typically situated near easily navigable rivers. Moreover, the continent was riddled with internal conflict. You also have to give credit to the Vikings' naval craftsmanship—only their boats could maneuver so easily in rivers.

As the Vikings primarily plundered monasteries, ports, and trading centers to increase their riches, when they realized they could profit even further from internal divisions in the continent, they soon decided to take advantage of this internal strife.

For example, in 840, when Louis the Pious (king of the Franks) died, a power struggle among his sons ensued. His eldest son, Lothair I, approached the Vikings for support against his brothers, which the Vikings were only happy to oblige. However, this only turned Viking attention onto Francia, and soon Frankish kings and rulers became hostage to the Norsemen—paying them to spare their towns and people.

Conquests, Exploration, and Settlement

THE BRITISH ISLES

By the mid-ninth century, the British Isles saw invasions of the Vikings. This time, however, they did settle. Territories in mainland England, Ireland and Scotland, the Hebrides, and Northern Islands in Scotland were claimed by the Vikings. Major Irish trading towns such as Dublin, Limerick, and Wexford were founded by the Vikings during this age of conquest. Much of Ireland was dominated by these clansmen, which they used as a base for conducting attacks on England from across the Irish Sea. The raids and conquests in England intensified in response to the fortifications which were occurring across the English Channel.

For the inhabitants of England, this was not good news. The kingdoms of East Anglia, Northumberland, and Mercia could not withstand an attack from the Vikings; their ranks composed mostly of Danes. The editors of Britannica provide more details on the conquest of these territories and kingdoms.

> [A] force led by the sons of Ragnar Lothbrok—Halfdan, Inwaer (Ivar the Boneless), and perhaps Hubba (Ubbe)—conquered the ancient kingdoms of East Anglia

and Northumbria and reduced Mercia to a fraction of its former size (The Editors of Britannica., 2020).

Such territorial expansions continued in the second half of the ninth century. The West Saxons were able to make two crucial comebacks against the Danes. First, at the Battle of Ashdown in 871, the King Æthelred and his younger brother and future king, Alfred the Great, met Viking commanders Bagsecg and Halfdan. Both the Viking commanders had been pivotal to the invasion of England (as mentioned in the above quote). The Battle of Ashdown saw a crucial victory to the West Saxons. On January 8th, the Vikings took formation at the top of the ridge, gaining advantage over the West Saxons. After their reconnaissance provided insight about Viking formation, the West Saxons copied theirs and charged up the hill. One of the crucial points that may have won the war for the West Saxons was when Æthelred later joined the battle. Since this strategy was based on surprise, it is considered the factor that won them the battle.

The second comeback for the West Saxons was during the Battle of Eddington. Under King Alfred the Great of Wessex, the West Saxons defeated a Danish/Viking army. In 878, the Battle of Edington took place, which saw the Viking army defeated by Alfred the Great's forces. Guthrum, the Danish warlord and king of East Anglia, surrendered, forcing him to agree to a treaty with Alfred the Great. Officially called The Treaty of Alfred and Guthrum, the terms applied to the Vikings was that the Danes could preside over certain territories in North and East England while others would remain under Anglo-Saxon control. Alfred the Great also named another condition: Guthrum would have to be baptized into the Christian faith. Keeping his oath until his death, Guthrum ruled over East Anglia under his baptized name Æthelstan. Up to this point Æthelred and Alfred the Great were the only English kings to withstand Norse conquest.

Despite the terms of the treaties, the Vikings had control over 15 shires in England including what is modern-day Buckingham, Derby, Essex, Leicester, Northampton, Suffolk, and York. These areas were called Danelaw, meaning that they followed Danish laws and codes as opposed to West-Saxon and Mercian Law.

During the decade of the 840s, inland cities such as Limoges and Nantes were targets for Viking attacks. Viking activity became intermittent for some time in the European continent. They attacked Sevilla which was under Arab rule in 844 and plundered Pisa in the Italian peninsula in 859. In the new century, they turned their attention to Francia once more.

Charles III, king of West Francia, ceded territory over to the Viking king Rouen in 911. The territory annexed was Normandy, taking its name from this original translation which means "land of the Northmen."

Their expansion from Scandinavia went even further, traveling north and west. In roughly 900, they set up colonies in Iceland. Hundreds of settlers poured into this distant island. They also began to populate Greenland. As mentioned, their adventures also took them to North America, more specifically, Newfoundland. Two Norse sagas exist explaining the finding of the New World. First, in 1000, Bjarni Herjólfsson—a Viking explorer—was traveling to Greenland when his boat was blown off course. The explorer spotted an unknown shoreline and returned home to share this news. A year later, Leif Erikson and 35 men went in search of the land that Bjarni Herjólfsson had spotted. Subsequent voyages by the Leif Brothers and Icelandic trader, Thorfinn Karlsefni, occurred for the next three years. There is archaeological evidence from L'Anse aux Meadows (a historic site in Newfoundland and Labrador) proving that the Vikings did voyage to and settle in North America. It is estimated that they traveled even further into the continent into the province of New Brunswick.

You have already read about Viking dominion in the Irish mainland. The Viking invasions of Ireland took place in about 795. They would continue to preside over most of the mainland, using it as a base to conduct warfare against the inhabitants of England. Though they controlled much of the territory such as Dublin—the Kingdom of Dublin under Viking rule—the Irish retained hold over some areas. The Dál gCais, an Irish Gaelic tribe, began to expand their kingdom in the 10th century. Their king, Brian Boru, led them to March on Dublin, which was under Viking control, and in 1014 the Irish went to war with the Vikings to reclaim their land. At the Battle of Clontarf in April 1014, even though Brian Boru died in the battle, his forces were victorious. Brian Boru has been recorded in Irish history as a hero, freeing the Irish from Viking and foreign domination.

Much focus has been placed on the Vikings as being raiders and plunderers. That they were. However, they were also explorers and traders. For a band of people who lived 1000 years ago, their desire to discover foreign lands seems endless. Their voyages took them to Kievan Rus (modern-day Ukraine), Constantinople, Iran and the Middle East, and Constantinople. They traded their furs in many of these regions.

Viking Culture, Religion, and Military

From Led Zeppelin's music to the popular *Vikings* television series, fascination about Viking culture has resurged in contemporary culture. Though we find their religion and means of conducting military fascinating, aspects of modern culture are rooted in theirs.

SEAFARING AND NAVAL CRAFTSMANSHIP

While the Vikings are known for their violent raids, before they could plunder they needed ships and boats. Thus, necessity drove the Vikings to become both excellent naval craftsmen and seafarers. They were also superb navigators. Although unproven, it's been suggested they used a tool called a 'sunstone'—a type of crystal allowing them to always track the location of the sun even during sunset or on overcast days.

Once again, it was a necessity that acted as a catalyst, driving the Vikings to advance maritime craft. Even in modern times, the Vikings are renowned for their 'longship' or 'longboat.' This vessel demonstrated true excellence in naval craftsmanship, as Dr. William Short explains.

> [Longships] had very shallow drafts ... strong enough to cross the open ocean, but they were shallow enough that they could go way up river and truly surprise people in places where no one expected ... [and they could] sail very close to the wind – atypical for European ships of that time

> ... sail[ing] in many directions, and unexpected directions given the wind (qtn in Walsh D., 2013)

Additionally, their longboats were built slim, allowing the Vikings to maneuver well in rivers. With this advantage, by 842 the Vikings attacked inland towns such as Limoges, Nantes, and Orleans. Even after the Viking Age ended, this type of ship continued to dominate Northern European waters, approximately being the predominant vessel for 1500 years in this region. Their longboats had fixed oars to the side of the boats, giving the Vikings more rowing power.

While not as ingrained in popular culture, the Vikings also had a different class of sea vessel—namely, the knarr. Unlike the longboat, the knarr was used for trading purposes. It had a broader design, did not use the same oars of the longboats, and was built to carry heavy cargo.

LANGUAGE AND LITERATURE

In the introduction, we explored how clues in modern language tell us about our culture and history. When the Vikings settled in the British Isles, they contributed to and shaped our language as well. For example, the days of the week such as 'Thursday'—day of Thor—and 'Friday'—day of Frigg or Freya. Specifically in the British Isles, there were other more noticeable contributions such as the names of villages and homesteads. Finally, very common words such as 'give' and 'window' come from Viking influence.

While there is not much archaeological evidence for all the exploits of the Norsemen, after the Viking Age during the 11th, 12th, and 13th centuries, numerous sagas were created recounting these adventures. As you have read, there are two about discovering North America, there are others about Erik the Red, Ragnar Lothbrok, and his sons Ivar the Boneless and Bjorn Ironside, and Gunnar Hamundarson.

Society and Culture

If you go back to the word '*vikingr*,' it strictly applied to men. This meant that women could not be Vikings. While this occurred in an official sense, it certainly was not true for everyday life. Using DNA evidence, researchers uncovered in 2014 that Norse women had joined the Viking men in their voyages to England, Iceland, and Ireland. In fact, Viking women were crucial to the settlement of Iceland, helping the settlement to thrive.

While it is true that Norse women had domestic duties such as raising children, they also had much freedom for a woman living 1000 years ago. For example, they could own property, ask for a divorce, and reclaim their dowries in the case of divorce. Though it was quite rare, women were also warriors or rather, 'shieldmaidens.' A Danish historian, Saxo Grammaticus, wrote during the 12th century that during the mid-eighth century Battle of Brávellir, 300 Viking women fought along with their men.

In some ways Viking culture was progressive, like the freedom enjoyed by its women. However, in other cases, it resembled other feudal societies present at the time. Norse society was divided into three classes: earls (*jarlar*), free men (*karlar*), and slaves (*þrælar*).

Jarlar were the chieftains and aristocrats who owned lands and generally were married. Land typically was inherited by the oldest or older sons. *Karlar* were typically young men who did not inherit land. As a result, they did not marry and labored on a portion of the land owned by the *jarlar*. Interestingly, it was this class of free men which composed the majority of Vikings. As there was little chance of social mobility and means of creating wealth, they typically went on sea voyages to plunder and obtain their own wealth.

There is a theory that it was the free men's need for wives and concubines which drove them to leave Scandinavia. It also could explain why Viking culture was violent as there was fierce competition among the men for wives. A medieval Irish text called the Annals of Ulster supports this theory.

Scandinavian practices that led powerful men to monopolize women also might have led to significant pools of unwed men ... Evolutionary biology suggests that such an imbalance would have then boosted competition for mates among unmarried men ... This resulted in volatile societies in Scandinavia in which men were moved to engage in risky behavior, such as raiding expeditions to gain wealth and status to attract brides and to secure female slaves. (Choi, C.Q., 2016)

The last group of Norse society were the slaves. They enjoyed little freedom. Sometimes, if their master died, the slaves would be killed and burnt with their master. Generally, slaves did farm work for their feudal landowners. Slaves could either be born slaves, could be captured in war—gained from raids conducted abroad like in Ireland, where Dublin became a central slaving trade hub—or if an individual went bankrupt.

WEAPONS

For Viking freemen or *karlar*, they were expected to own weapons and carry them on their persons at all times. From the Norse sagas and laws of the 13th century, we learn that a significant amount of social status was attached to weapons. For example, a wealthier individual would have a full collection of arms and armor including a helmet, sword, mail shirt, and shield.

If we compare the Viking soldiers with those of the Bulgars, more status was placed on men-at-arms—those bearing swords. Though ranged melee was commonplace during the opening stages of battle, archery was considered less honorable than hand-to-hand combat.

The Second Viking Age

Towards the end of the 10th century, the Second Viking Age is said to have begun. It started when Sweyn Forkbeard led a rebellion against his father, Harald Bluetooth (2)—who was the king of a unified and Christianized Denmark—and seized power from his father. From this first act of rebellion, Forkbeard achieved what no other Viking king had managed: becoming the King of England. From 986 to 1014, Forkbeard was crowned King of Denmark, England, and Norway.

John of Wallingford, a Benedictine monk of St. Albans, chronicles Sweyn Forkbeard's invasion of England. It is said to have commenced in 1002 and ended in 1013, where Forkbeard managed to take the throne. The catalyst for the invasion was St Brice's Massacre which ordered the killing of Danes by the illy-advised king Æthelred II, more famously known as Æthelred the Unready.

In 1013, Forkbeard instructed a full-on invasion of the country, which saw Æthelred the Unready fleeing to Normandy (northwest France). That year Forkbeard became king of England. However, his death the next year saw his son, Harald II, succeed him as King of Denmark while his younger son, Canute, was declared King of England. Æthelred the Unready returned from Normandy to challenge the latter's ascension to the throne. The Vikings were driven out by Æthelred the Unready and his forces, but two years later, Canute retaliated and was again crowned king of England, Denmark, Norway, and parts of Sweden.

Canute's place on the throne—or as he was also known, Canute the Great—was challenged by a group of rebels led by Harald Hardrada who sought to restore King Olaf II to the throne in Norway. Harald Hardrada and his brother's plans failed, resulting in the death of Olaf at the Battle of Stiklestad in 1030 (see cover image). Attention then turned to England. There was an agreement between Magnus and Harthacnut to invade the island and once again restore Danish rule in the land. Magnus died and Harald Hardrada took up his claim. Joining forces with the Northumbrian king Tostig Godwinson, Hardrada pillaged coastal towns. Tostig Godwinson was hoping to reclaim his titles and land from King Harold Godwinson, Tostig's ambitious brother. The King, Godwinson, was of Viking descent, so the Battle of Stamford Bridge saw Viking against Viking, brother against brother.

Throughout September 1066, Hardrada and Tostig forces pillaged and burned down towns in Northumbria forcing people to surrender. On September 25th, the anticipated Battle of Stamford Bridge took place. Harald had expected a win, but in the end King Harold Godwinson was victorious.

Any hope Tostig and Hardrada had of regaining England was extinguished three weeks later. At the Battle of Hastings the Norman Duke, William the Conqueror, met King Harold Godwinson. William the Conqueror lived up to his name and annexed England, becoming the ruler of England. The Viking Age had ended; the Norman one had begun.

While the Viking Age is said to have ended with the Norman Invasion of 1066, from a cultural perspective the end coincides with a so-called death of Viking culture. By 1066, most Vikings had been Christianized, their polytheistic religion abandoned. Other aspects of Viking culture were absorbed into England and Scandinavia, forever leaving their mark on the language and culture of Christian Europe. Nonetheless, Scandinavian scholars were determined that the sagas of the greatest Viking heroes remain alive in public imagination. Though the end of the Viking Age came abruptly, Scandinavian scholars kept their tales alive in the 11th, 12th, and 13th centuries.

CHAPTER EIGHT

CAROLINGIAN EMPIRE

C. 800–888 CE

The Carolingian Dynasty may have endured for less than a century, but thanks to the campaigns of Charlemagne, this dynasty achieved what no other empire did after the Roman Empire: bringing most of Western Europe under one ruler. In fact, Charlemagne annexed parts of Europe that eluded the Roman Empire, earning him the title 'Father of Europe.'

To add to the Carolingian Dynasty's achievements was also the survival of Christianity and its growing influence in the continent but at the same time a revival of Pagan antiquities. The short reign of the Carolingian dynasty left its mark on Europe. Its decay began soon after the death of Charlemagne and though it was clearly rotting, the dynasty endured until 888. In this chapter, we will look at how Charlemagne became the Father of Europe, through reviewing the dynasty's expansion, introduction of unique policies and codes, its culture and analyzing why it began to crumble soon after.

Background

Like many medieval empires, their catalyst was the collapse of the Roman Empire. A group of Germanic peoples called the Franks occupied the region between the rivers Loire and Rhine. When the Great Migration Period of the early Middle Ages ended, Francia—the kingdom of the Franks—was established.

In 843, this kingdom was split into three parts: West Francia, Middle Francia, and East Francia. West Francia is what is now modern-day France, East Francia contemporary Germany, and Middle Francia, wedged right between the two, is currently where the Netherlands, Luxembourg, and Switzerland are located (1).

Though Francia was accepted as a kingdom, it was an aristocratic family responsible for the decision-making. The king's office became entirely ceremonial. Instead, it was the Mayor of the Palace who held true power—in this case, specifically the Merovingian Dynasty. From the Basque Country in Spain to the Rhine, the Merovingians had previously conquered and established their rule from the 5th to 8th century.

During most of that time, the second Merovingian king's sons divided Francia among themselves, creating four separate kingdoms: Austrasia, Neustria, Burgundy, and Aquitaine. Like we saw with the Lombard kingdom, internal conflict and division acted as a catalyst for political instability. In Francia, betrayal was common; alliances popped up to serve short-term needs, only to end just as quickly again. The Merovingian Dynasty further weakened their empire as they were pushing for the Mayor of the Palace to have more power; the King of the Franks became increasingly ceremonial. Britannica reveals the true amount of authority this figure commanded.

> The Merovingian kings adopted the system by which great landowners of the Roman Empire had employed a major domus (mayor, or supervisor, of the household) to superintend the administration of numerous, often scattered, estates. The Merovingians appointed a major palatii (mayor of the palace) to perform a similar function. The mayor gradually acquired further duties and powers: he obtained authority over court personnel, advised the king on the appointment of counts and dukes, protected the commendati (persons commended to the king) and the

king's wards, and eventually even came to command the royal army. (The Editors of Britannica, 2012)

Rise of the Carolingian Dynasty

CHARLES MARTEL

Martel was an illegitimate son of Pepin II or Pepin of Herstal, whose lineage could be traced to the Pepinids and Arnulfings, families from modern-day Belgium. With Pepin II, these two families were united. At his wife's request, Pippin II was asked to remove his sons Martel and Childebrand as his successors. Though both of his sons had already died, Plectrude—Pepin II's wife—aimed for their grandson to become the next Mayor of the Palace.

After Pepin II's death in 714, Theuodold took on the role. It did not sit well with the Austrasians as he was only eight years old then. Martel contested Theuodold's succession. In what was a sign of things to expect later, Charles Martel demonstrated much militaristic capability. He rose in popularity among the Austrasians owing to his successful campaigns. Theuodold and his mother were not willing to let go of power. What ensued was a civil war lasting three years.

The King of the Franks, acting in a more ceremonial position, named his own successor, Ragenfrid: the Mayor of the Palace for both Neustria and Burgundy. This was reason enough to meet Theuodold in battle, where the latter was slain. Meanwhile, Martel escaped from prison where he had been sent on Plectrude's orders. On escaping, he revived his ambition of becoming Mayor of the Palace in Austrasia. In March 717, Martel, after gathering forces from Liège, invaded Neustria, ending in a victory for Martel.

EXPANSION UNDER CHARLES MARTEL

Charles Martel or *Carolus Martellus* served as the Austrasian Mayor of the Palace from 715 to 741 and the Neustrian one from 718 to 741. Though he wielded much power in this role, it was the iconic Battle of Tours where he garnered much more recognition. Even Edward Gibbon, the historian who believed the light on Europe ended after the Roman Empire's fall, named Charles Martel "the name the paramount prince of his age" for his dashing heroism in this battle. Aquitaine was an independent region at the time, yet they encountered hostility from the Umayyad Caliphate to the South. The Burgundian duke, Odo, had little choice but to ask Martel for help against this attack, to which Martel agreed on the condition of Burgundian submission. This iconic battle ended in a victory to the Franks, helping Martel expand his borders.

While Martel never took the title of king, he was involved with Austrasia's territorial expansion. Almost immediately on taking office as Mayor of the Palace, Martel became involved in a series of wars spanning from 718 to 732. He led wars against the Saxons, the Frisians, Agilolfing dukes in Bavaria, and Alemannia. West Frisia (now in The Netherlands), Southern Germany, as well as Northern Germany were added to Francia. On his death in 741, the kingdom was once more split among the sons, Carloman and Pepin the Short.

Name Origins

Officially, the Carolingian Dynasty began with Pepin II who served as the Mayor of the Palace. Officially, the *empire* is said to have begun with Charlemagne in 800. What makes the Carolingian Dynasty unique is that there are specific dates signifying its beginning and end. On Christmas Day at Rome's Basilica, the empire is said to have begun when the Pope crowned Charlemagne *Imperator Romanorum*. The foundations of this empire began with Martel, continuing with his heir and son, Pepin the Short, and also with Martel's grandson, Charlemagne.

Like with many ruling positions in medieval times, they were hereditary. The name Carolingian comes from the obvious dynastic approach to ruling—the family name, Charles: first with Charles Martel, then with Charlemagne (literally translating to Charles the Great), and towards the end with Charles the Bald and Charles the Fat.

Pepin the Short

Not as well known as his father, Charles Martel, nor his son, Charlemagne, Pepin the Short nevertheless had some significant accomplishments influencing the Carolingian Dynasty and Francia's future. After his father's death, the two sons, Carloman and Pepin the Short ruled as Mayors of the Palace—Pepin over Neustria, Burgundy, and Provence, and Carloman over Austrasia, Alemania, and Thuringia. Where Martel failed to be named a Frankish king, Pepin did not. After naming Childeric III king of the Franks and Carloman retiring in 747 to enter a life in the monastery, allowed Pepin to consolidate his power and act as Mayor of the Palace and *dux et princeps Francorum* over all of Frankish territories. Pepin soon dispensed with Childeric III, forcing him to a monastic life in 751.

France may have lost its king in 751, but Pepin took up the mantle soon afterwards, declaring himself the King of the Franks. Certainly, it was in some sense a betrayal of Childeric III on Pepin's part, but Pepin's betrayal created a dynastic line for the kingdom. The role of Mayor of the Palace now merged with that of the king.

Another achievement of Pepin was that he managed to move closer with the Papacy, influencing the dynasty's future. One of the first major actions Pepin took as king was to go to war with Lombards. He was the first to do so. This allowed him to draw closer to Papal states as he forced the Lombard king, Aistulf, to give up Ravenna and Pentapolis. While Pepin was not known as much for his territorial expansion, he did allow Francia to grow, focusing on Aquitaine. Though he resorted to brutal tactics like setting fire to much of the region, important cities such as Toulouse did fall to Pepin in 767.

Father of Europe

In 768, Charlemagne co-ruled with his brother Carloman after their father died, thus inheriting the title of King of the Franks. Born in 742 in Aachen (now in Germany), Charlemagne (also *Karolus Magnus*), literally translating to Charles the Great, would live up to his name by expanding Frankish territory to found the Carolingian Empire, bringing about the Carolingian Renaissance and introducing reforms allowing Christianity to survive to contemporary Europe.

Though Pepin set up a joint inheritance of Francia, Charlemagne was about 26 years old when he succeeded his father; Carloman was only 17. For years, Charlemagne served by his father's side, making him a competent military leader and fighter. Like their predecessors, Charlemagne and his brother, Carloman, had specific territories under their authority. Under Charlemagne was Neustria, Northern Austrasia, and Western Aquitaine while Carloman ruled over Septimania, Southern Austrasia, Burgundy, Provence, Swabia, some regions on the Italian border, and Eastern Aquitaine.

This split of Aquitaine would end up bringing not only division in the province but among the two ruling brothers. Split leadership, as well as cultural and linguistic divisions, sparked a rebellion between the Aquitanians and Gascons in 769 in Aquitaine. As it fell under the rule of both brothers, Charlemagne, with the help of his brother, planned to meet Hunald II, the Duke of Aquitaine, with his army in battle—except that Carloman fled to Burgundy, leaving Charlemagne to fight on his own. The victory went to Francia. Carloman had returned with his army to aid his brother's, but this only inspired further animosity between the brothers. At the age of 20, in 771, Carloman died, leaving the entire kingdom in Charlemagne's hands. Even to this day, it remains unclear if on Carloman's death whether the co-ruler should inherit the territories or if they were to go to Carloman's heirs. What we do know is that Charlemagne became the single ruler and king of the Franks in December 771.

TERRITORIAL EXPANSION

With the rebellion quashed in Aquitaine, Charlemagne's first plan was to expand Frankish dominion. Once Aquitaine submitted to the Frankish king, Gascony became Charlemagne's first territorial acquisition. For the next decades of his rule, Charlemagne continued to expand his frontiers. Often events took place which favored Charles the Great's imperial ambitions.

The most obvious example was the Saxon Wars, spanning 30 years of conflict. The Saxons were a confederate of Germanic tribes, settled in Northeast Germany. Despite Charlemagne being a devout Christian leader and the Saxons being Pagan, for decades the Saxons and Franks enjoyed amicable relations, facilitating trade between the Franks, Saxons, and Scandinavians. Nonetheless, the Pagan beliefs of his neighbor irked Charlemagne. Such tensions came to boiling point in 772. The Saxons sacked and burned a church in Deventer (in the Netherlands). This brought out the wrath of Charlemagne whose retribution involved destroying Irminsul, a sacred tree integral to Norse beliefs. Some historians point out that war with the Saxons was an opportune moment for Charlemagne to act on his political agenda to once again expand his territory. The following paragraph sheds light on the potential political motive.

> The Carolingian actions against the Saxons fit neatly into ideas of what imperial duties and responsibilities meant in Western Europe, chief among them which was to protect the Catholic church and expand the faith. Charlemagne and his administration were keen to promote this fact, especially to the Papacy. At the same time, Popes Adrian I (772-795) and Leo III (795-816) were also eager to encourage the Carolingians to carry out this task (Medievalists, 2014).

The results of the events brought 30 years of wars between the two peoples. Whether religion was at the heart of Carolingian expansion, it was used as a cover for some brutal attacks. One particularly memorable event was the Massacre of Verden, where Charlemagne ordered 4500 Saxons to be beheaded. From annal collections (2), we learn the Saxons, under their leader Widukind, staged a rebellion in October 782, winning the Battle of Süntel. When Charlemagne arrived at the confluence of rivers Aller and Wester, he ordered the deaths of those Saxons. The Frankish king hoped for Christian conversion, but the massacre of Verden was another instance of the brutal approach used.

For the next two decades, the Saxons remained unbreakable and unshakeable. Then in the early 800s, Charlemagne instructed 10,000 Saxons to be moved to Neustria and 10,000 Frankish to move into former Saxon territory. Saxony was then absorbed into Carolingian territory.

Another formidable foe for the Franks were the Basques in Spain. Charlemagne suffered a significant defeat at the Battle of Roncevaux Pass to the Basques in 778. The Franks lost many soldiers and the war had been costly, including losing the invaluable Frankish commander, Roland, making Charlemagne wary of invading Spain again. In fact, Charlemagne was so wary of battle again with the Basques that he set up Marca Hispanica, a buffer region between France and Spain, as well as instructing Carolingian officials to oversee the Pyrenees and to alert the king of any movements into Frankish territory. Eventually, in the next decade, the Carolingian Empire added Barcelona. Some territories such as Zaragoza evaded Charlemagne's capture and remained in the hands of the Muslims, but not all. The Frankish king managed to annex Sardinia, Corsica, and the Balearic Islands from the Moors, or Saracens as they were known at the time.

Lastly, we cannot forget Charlemagne's standoffs with the Lombards. Friendship with the Lombards had been short. Charles the Great married Desiderius' daughter in 770 when he was approximately 28. Several months later, he rejected Desiderata and married the teenage Swabian Hildegard. With Desiderata returned to her father, relations soured understandably between the two kingdoms. Once again this worked in favor with Charlemagne, who by creating hostility between the Franks and the Lombards, deliberately fostered closer ties with the Papacy. Pavia, the capital city of the Lombards, was captured, most of Longobardia Major was assimilated, and Charlemagne was crowned King of the Franks and Lombards.

Despite fighting battles in every direction, this did little to dissuade Charlemagne from expanding to the east. In fact, it is likely that Charlemagne sought to replicate the might of the Roman Empire, making invasion in Eastern Europe attractive. In 788, Bavaria sat at Francia's limits, vulnerable to attack and prompting Charlemagne to travel to Bavaria to secure their borders, which really meant extending them. The Avars, an alliance of Eurasian nomads and Turkic peoples, tried negotiating peace with their Frankish neighbors, but the Franks went ahead with their plans of founding the Avar March. It was a Frankish state that over time increased in size, absorbing territories from the river Enns to the Vienna Woods and the Danube. These new additions were under the supervision of a Bavarian official, Gerold, who was responsible for securing the borders between Bavaria and Pannonia.

Clearly, the Carolingian Kingdom ceased long ago to be a kingdom or a dynasty. After conquering so many territories and assimilating so many different peoples and cultures, the Carolingian Empire was one except in name until in 800, when Pope Leo III crowned Charlemagne as the first Holy Roman Emperor. After suffering an attack from Romans, the Pope fled to Paderborn in the German Rhineland. Swearing an oath to Charlemagne and seeking his assistance in restoring him as pope in Rome, Pope Leo III and Charlemagne became even more closely aligned. On Christmas Day of 800, Charlemagne was crowned *Imperator Romanorum* (the Roman Emperor) and the Carolingian Empire was founded.

As mentioned, Charlemagne is considered the first Holy Roman Emperor. Some historians contest, stating that Empress Irene of Byzantium was already the Roman Ruler of the time. It could have been a political move on the Pope's part. Already then, the East-West or Catholic-Orthodox Schism was in its infancy, sparked by the iconoclast values of the Orthodox church in Byzantium. Historians are unsure whether Charlemagne knew in advance of his coronation or whether he even wrote to the pope asking for it. What is clear is that the Carolingian Empire was born—and I daresay the first Holy Roman Emperor was crowned.

MILITARY STRENGTH

Charles the Great would have always been great. One reason for being so was the sheer strength of the Frankish army during the eighth and early ninth centuries. First, the army consisted of about 30,000 soldiers. It is by no means a huge army by today's standards, but back then it was impressive. The second aspect of French strength we will read about in the next chapter in more detail: Frankish heavy cavalry. As opposed to light cavalry, these knights were clad in chain mail and bore shields. They also went through years of training, making them hard to fight against and even tougher to reproduce for counterattacks.

Tactics also came into play. Significant Medieval battles such as the Battle of the Catalaunian Plains and Battle of Hastings generally took the long-pitched form, meaning that generals deployed their men in the location and once both were prepared, they engaged in conflict. Charlemagne preferred skirmishes. Certainly, such ambushes can be deadly, but their scope is limited. However, if a tribe or kingdom faces too many deadly skirmishes they can weaken over time, making it tough to stave invasion off in the long run. To complement such an approach, Charlemagne planned battles long in advance and especially during Easter, when harvests were carried out, meaning that granaries were full. With a surplus of food, Charlemagne's forces could engage in raid after raid on all frontiers.

CAROLINGIAN RENAISSANCE

In 772, when the Saxons burned down a church, the church had been created by an English missionary, Lebuinus. Lebuinus' faith might have been influenced by Anglican beliefs, but when the church was burned down, Charlemagne's retribution was provoked. Though Charlemagne's reprisal against the Saxon paganistic belief was without question brutal, there was religious intolerance to some extent throughout the empire, especially with the Moors' Muslim faith. The Islamic World had been making strides in astronomy, alchemy (3), and mathematics since the Roman Empire's fall. Despite the religious intolerance, Charlemagne was an avid supporter of learning and education, welcoming wherever possible advances in knowledge and science, even if originating from outside of Christendom. Britannica provides more insight:

> From Moorish Spain came Christian refugees who also contributed to this intellectual revival; disputations with the Muslims had forced them to develop a dialectic skill in which they now instructed Charlemagne's subjects (The Editors of Britannica, 2022).

The Carolingian Renaissance centered around Christianity, with the goal of creating Christendom. Charlemagne believed greater exposure to Christian ideals, an increase in scholarly endeavors, and reforms in the church would allow the kingdom's subjects to become better Christians and lead more moral lives. Medieval texts such as *Admonitio generalis* and *Epistola de litteris colendis*, collected by Charlemagne (4) in the late 8th century, reveal that the king saw himself as a kind of new Constantine, tasked with the role of increasing the spread of Christianity. Like Constantine, Charlemagne introduced a number of reforms to the faith's institutions.

One was education. Charlemagne believed that Catholic leaders should learn Latin so that they could correctly interpret the Biblical canon. This not only promoted greater learning among Christian adherents but also "educational reform bore fruit in a generation of churchmen whose morals and whose education were of a higher standard than before" (The Editors of Britannica, 2022). Another was architecture. Influenced by Romanesque architecture, monasteries and abbeys tended to be built with arches or in the Basilican form. Some examples include the Palatine Chapel in Aachen, a chapel containing numerous rooms and appendices, typical of Basilican style.

While the educational reforms had some advantages, there were linguistic changes made which had some serious downsides. To make a quick digression, often you will see the languages such as Spanish, Portuguese, French, and Italian being referred to as Romance languages. This is not because they are romantic, but because they derive from the Roman Empire. During Charlemagne, Romance—kinds of dialects of Latin—separated further from Latin, leading to a new form of Ecclesiastical Latin being created. The problem is that few adherents could follow or speak this form of Latin, often referred to as "Church Latin" as their native language was a Romance dialect (Wright, R., 1982). Therefore, the majority of the population could not take part in the intellectual and linguistic development which occurred during Charlemagne's reign.

Before the Euro currency was introduced in 2002, Charlemagne was years ahead of the European Union. In response to a shortage of gold, the emperor introduced a new currency called *livre carolinienne*, which was used in much of the continent, streamlining trade. Furthermore, fiscal principles forced the individuals to record all their expenses according to new accounting systems implemented.

There were a number of administrations implemented during Charlemagne's time. As we read about earlier with Gerold, who oversaw the Avar March, he functioned as a Bavarian prefect in the frontier unit. This function of Gerold indicates that the empire was divided into two sections: the core empire and its frontier units, known as *Regna*. Austrasia, Burgundy, and Neustria constituted the core, which was ruled over directly by Charlemagne. Both Italy and Aquiaine were made into separate kingdoms over which his sons, Pepin of Italy and Louis the Pious, ruled over respectively. The main functions of prefects in the *Renga* included fortifying the border and preparing for any sudden invasions.

Decline

Territorial expansion occurred until Charlemagne's death. When Pepin of Italy took over supplanting the Lombards, he attempted to expand the empire, but was met with little success. One of his most disastrous campaigns was Venice, which saw the death of many soldiers to disease native to the swamplands. After six months, the campaign was abandoned and Pepin died soon after in 810.

Things were not looking better for Louis the Pious. His rule over the core Frankish empire was riddled with civil wars throughout the 830s—not to mention the numerous frontier wars that left a population displaced. There were some further attempts to expand the empire into Longobardia Minor, but they too were fruitless. In 840, Louis the Pious died after falling ill.

According to Mayke de Jong, studying Medieval empires in Utrecht University, the Carolingian empire was always in a state of decline. This may be true while Charlemagne ruled, but it was certainly true after he died. The clearest evidence for this was not only the split among his three grandsons, Lothar, Charles, and Louis, but the internal division among them. After three years of civil war and a year of negotiations, the Treaty of Verdun was signed allocating the middle Frankish kingdom to Lothar I, the East Frankish Kingdom to Louis II, and the West Frankish Kingdom to Charles II. Though Charles the Fat managed to briefly unite the empire under one ruler, the Treaty of Verdun was instrumental in bringing dissent and division in the empire and failing to bring the peace it promised.

> The treaty was not governed by geographical factors but was an attempt to satisfy the claims of each brother for a share in the Carolingian family estates, many of which were in the fertile lands of the middle kingdom, Lotharingia. Lotharingia soon lost its own identity and became a battleground for the embryonic kingdoms of France and Germany (Treaty of Verdun, 2022).

The third civil war occurred in Germany, as Louis II revolted against Louis' move crowning Charles ruler over Alemannia. Not only did the empire have to contend with internal conflict but frontier wars too. Rebellions became commonplace, causing portions of the population to become displaced, especially in the *Regna*. Mayke de Jong concludes the dramatic end of the Carolingian empire, stating "it was something of a relief that the last legitimate emperor, aptly named Charles the Fat, was deposed in 888" (de Jong, M., 2015).

The Carolingian Dynasty might have had a short existence—the empire an even shorter one—but they certainly left their mark on Europe. Their two impactful leaders, Charles Martel and Charlemagne, demonstrated that one powerful family could influence the future of a continent. The empire's territory expanded to dimensions of the Roman Empire in less than a century. Yet, it also took less than a century for the kingdom to disintegrate. What Charles Martel and Charlemagne managed to achieve left a much longer mark on the continent: the expansion of Christendom, Christian reform, efficient military practices, and administrative efficacy.

CHAPTER NINE
THE NORMANS
c. 911–1485

Viking influence in Europe did not end in 1066. It could be argued that it came with renewed vigor when William the Conqueror annexed England and crowned himself the King of England.

William the Conqueror, the Duke of Normandy, was a living manifestation of the new form which Viking culture and strength took on. Normandy—translating to "Land of the Northmen"—took its name from the original Viking conquest in France.

Over time, the Vikings integrated with the local Franks, forming a unique Norman state which would irk and contest that of the Byzantine and Ottoman empires, shape the future of Great Britain and Europe, blend with Anglo-Saxon ultimately giving rise to the English language, and develop an Empire that would endure for a half a millennium.

Norman Beginnings and Kingdom of the Franks

The Vikings not only tormented England, but France too. Eventually the Anglo-Saxons drove out the Vikings. However, the Franks did not achieve the same. This left the Gallo-Franks little choice but to pay the Viking invaders off and cede territory to them to prevent further pillaging.

In 911, Charles the Simple gave Rouen and the surrounding area to a Viking chief named Rollo the Walker (1). With the Treaty of St. Clair-sur-Epte, Charles the Simple named conditions to Rollo on relinquishing the territory: conversion to Catholicism, an end to their pillaging and looting, and to protect the King of the Franks when called upon. Rollo agreed to the Frankish king's demands. Subsequently, Rollo converted to Christianity and was declared a vassal of Normandy. And so, the Duchy of Normandy was born.

Unlike their rivals across the Channel, after the Carolingian Dynasty ended, France was broken up into different duchies known as fiefs (2). Overseeing them all was the King of the Franks, located in the Northeast in the area known then as the *Domanie Royal* (Royal Domain). At the time, there was more centralized control over the whole country of England, but France did not exist as a unified country until the 13th century. Though the rulers of each Duchy swore loyalty to the crown, each ruler had much independence to control his territory as he saw fit. Like Rollo, the rulers of these fiefs were known as vassals.

The system of the fiefdoms in 10th-century France was based on feudalism like many other empires during the time. The King of the Franks ceded territories over to various vassals, like Rollo in Normandy. If, however, the crown required an army, the King of the Franks could always call upon the army of the different duchies for protection. That being said, each fiefdom enjoyed much autonomy, meaning that the ruler could make decisions outside the influence of the Crown.

The Normans: Culture, Religion, and Military

EMERGENCE OF A NORMAN CULTURE

As a Viking colony, Normandy became one of the strongest fiefs. Soon after establishing Viking control in the region, the Vikings brutally quashed any rebellion. As a result, Normandy enjoyed much stability, unlike other Frankish duchies. Despite their brutal put down of revolts, the Vikings also integrated themselves with the local Frankish culture. For example, they converted to Catholicism, adopted the language, respected French Law, and intermarried with the locals. Furthermore, land often remained under the control of French lords or knights fostering trust with the Frankish population. In the 11th century, it was clear that a hybrid of Viking and Frankish culture was emerging, giving rise to a new class of people: the Normans.

Their leader, Richard I (*Richard sans Peur*, meaning Richard Without Fear) is credited with creating a cohesive ethnic group and fiefdom from 942 to 996. Richard the Fearless became the first official duke of Normandy, though it was no simple matter. After the death of William Longsword, Richard I was destined to take over. However, Richard I was only 10 years old when his father died. The Frankish King, Louis IV, used his influence as king to have Richard I raised in the *Domanie Royal*. With Richard I in the Frankish kingdom, Louis IV seized Normandy. However, when Richard I was 14, he struck back. Using his Viking connections—being the grandson of Rollo—he was supported by the Normans and Viking Franks in Normandy as well as King Harold of Denmark. In 946, Richard I with his support captured Louis IV and forced him to recognize Normandy as its own fiefdom.

Under his son, Richard the Good, the Norman empire continued to expand in Frankish territory. From the 10th to 11th centuries, with Rollo and his ancestors William Longsword, Richard the Fearless, Richard the Good, Richard III, Robert the Magnificent, and William the Conqueror, the size of Normandy doubled. Lower Normandy was added to the region and the capital city was moved to Caen. While these leaders had a taste for conquest, they often made important political moves to cement their support in Normandy and with other Frankish duchies. For example, Richard the Good managed to form an alliance with both the King of the Franks and the Duchy of Brittany. In the case of the latter, the Norman duke married the Duke of Brittany's sister, helping create an alliance between Brittany and Normandy against the aggression of Burgundy. Richard the Good became officially recognized as the first Duke of Normandy. Another instrumental factor which allowed Normandy to enjoy much stability was handing over territory to Frankish knights and lords. This meant feudalism expanded under the Normans, allowing the Duchy to prosper and enjoy stability.

MILITARY

As we read in Chapter 7, the Vikings were mainly composed of infantry and some archers. During the late 9th and early 10th centuries, a new form of conducting warfare was occurring in France which gave the Franks and Normans an advantage over other nations, namely, the creation of Knights or *Les Chevaliers*.

Two key inventions took place during the time which allowed such an innovation in warfare to take place. First, there was the invention of the stirrup. Michael Fordham explains how crucial this invention was, revealing: "It allowed knights not only to charge their enemies on horseback, but to remain on the horse leaning out and swinging their swords while still fixed firmly in the saddle" (Fordham, M., 2017). Calvary or knights were deadly in combat. Not only could they move easily, but a banner of knights was particularly lethal when charging down a legion.

Second, *Les Chevaliers* enjoyed more protection with the introduction of the kite shield. Unlike round shields which were bulky and awkward, the almond-shaped kite shields offered full-body protection. Moreover, the shield was strapped to the knight's arm, allowing the warrior to dexterously defend themselves while remaining seated and fighting his opponent. The origins of the kite shield are unclear, but there are some historians who propose that it came from Viking influence. Whether this is true or not, what is known is that the kite shield became key to Norman military tactics.

During the 1050s, English king Edward the Confessor tried to train English knights against the Welsh. This backfired badly. Knights were advanced fighters. Not in a matter of years could the English master this new form of conflict. It took an immensely long time for knights to be sufficiently trained. Thus, the Normans and French had this advantage over other nations or empires.

Religion

No longer were the Vikings in Normandy pagans, but French-speaking Christians. As mentioned, the adoption of this religion was a political move. They had not only won the local population over but also the pope in Rome. One thing that brought such an alliance about was that the Normans had specifically adopted Roman Catholicism, as opposed to Christian Orthodoxy. They also began to build monasteries and churches in stone following a Romanesque design, such as building large arches in these religious buildings. One such example is the Abbe aux Dames of Caen, an abbey in the capital city. It was constructed after the pope permitted William the Conqueror to marry his first cousin, Mathilde of Flanders. This abbey, like many churches built during the time, won favor with the pope. Where the Normans grew in papal appreciation, the English (Anglo-Saxons) only seemed to draw contempt from the pope. With the exception of Westminster Abbey, most Anglo-Saxon churches were made from wood. It also did not help matters that, though the archbishops were under papal authority, the Anglo-Saxon archbishops did not follow orders from this authority. For instance, the Archbishop of Canterbury, Stigand, was named Archbishop of Canterbury but held onto his position as Bishop of Winchester, going directly against papal orders.

CASTLE BUILDING

In the 11th century, castles began to take the form of what we know them as today. Before the new millennium, in England and France they were largely wooden structures. Like their churches, the Normans began to construct stone castles. However, before they made this transition, there were two types of castles: the ringwork and motte-and-bailey types.

Though the ringwork design was simple, it was extensively used by the Normans during the 11th and 12th centuries. Like its name, a ring or circle made up its frame. First, the circular frame was wooden, but it evolved to stone. It was further protected by a ditch that was dug around it. Often, there were wooden towers constructed into the ramparts to increase the ringwork's defense.

While ringworks replaced motte-and-bailey castles, the latter too were improved. A motte-and-bailey involved a keep being built on a raised mound or hill (the motte). This keep would overlook the surrounding area, providing protection. In fact, workers would rush to dig the mound and build the keep and then build the remainder of the castle's structure, a walled courtyard (the bailey). Raids were common, so finishing the keep was a priority as it would protect them from invaders. Jean de Colmieu, a Provençal nobleman, reveals in the 13th century that in the department of Calais, the motte-and-bailey design was in use. In the 13th century, a stone keep was built as opposed to a wooden one, adding a further layer of protection.

Norman Expansion

Like their Viking ancestors, the Normans had a taste for expansion. The increase of their territory within Frankish lands was not enough to satiate their desire for expansion. They soon moved beyond Frankish-Gallo territory.

ITALY

Amatus of Montecassino, a Benedictine monk living during the 11th century, best-known for *L'Ystoire de li Normant* (chronicles of Norman history), is one of the chief sources that chronicled the Norman invasion of Southern Italy. What we learn from Amatus of Montecassino is that there were two Norman sieges in Bari and Salerno. Melus of Bari, a Lombard aristocrat, sought the help of the Normans against the Byzantines. What ensued was a divergence of Norman families, one backing the Lombards and the other—Hauteville and Drengot families—backing the Byzantines. During the early 11th century, Melus of Bari was defeated. The Hautevilles and Drengots were handsomely rewarded with titles and land. For reinstating the Byzantine Prince, Prince Guaimar IV of Salerno, in Apulia and Calabria, the former was awarded the count of Melfi and the latter the principality of Capua.

Similarly to their Viking predecessors who used Ireland as a base for the English conquest, the Normans used Melfi and Capua as military bases for further expansion, eventually capturing Malta and Sicily who were in the hands of Arabs then. The Hauteville family would annex Sicily, and Roger II would be crowned their king. Owing to its various inhabitants, the kingdom of Sicily would be a medieval melting pot blending Byzantine, Lombard, Norman, and Arabian traditions. From 1135 to 1160, the kingdom of Sicily was used as a base for the Norman empire to extend its reach into North Africa. Parts of medieval Algeria, Tunisia, and Libya were added to the kingdom of Sicily, but later lost in the second half of the century.

IBERIA

The Crusades brought a lot of activity to the Iberian Peninsula as well as the Holy Land. Owing to their good relations with the papacy, it was just a matter of time before the Normans too traveled to such areas. In the early 10th century, Barcelonese in northeast Spain suffered raids from the Andalusian caliphate. The Normans backed Barcelona. A century later, a Norman Knight, Robert Burdet, was involved in a revolt in the Ebro Basin (close to Catalonia). For his assistance, Burdet was given the principality of Tarragona (a city near Barcelona) which remained semi-autonomous. With the second conquest, Anglo-Normans continued to back the Iberians, such as the Portuguese King Afonso Henriques in the Siege of Lisbon in 1142. Although unsuccessful, a second siege in 1147 gave victory to the Portuguese, and many Normans settled into the fallen city. The conflict in the peninsula saw the Normans handsomely rewarded with territory during this time.

BYZANTIUM

This is almost to be expected. Byzantine territories were a hotspot for Medieval empires who were seeking expansion. At the time of the Norman invasion in Southern Italy, Byzantium was in a state of decline. Though the Normans acted as mercenaries for the Byzantines, when Roger I took over as count of Sicily, Byzantium lost all territory in Southern Italy. Inspired further by their success in Southern Italy, under Roger's elder brother, Robert Guiscard in the 1080s, the Normans continued to invade Byzantine territories such as Dyrrhachium (now Albania) and Corfu. During the siege of Dyrrhachium, the city of Larissa was lost. On the Byzantine side, there were many defeats, but 1085 brought a reversal of fortunes. Guiscard died. The Byzantine emperor, Alexios I Komnenos, sought help from Germanic mercenaries, and the Normans were defeated.

Half a century later, Roger II renewed the Norman attack, aiming to retake Corfu and capture Thebes and Corinth. The invasion was unsuccessful. Roger II retreated. Since the Byzantines created a formidable alliance with Conrad III of Germany, Norman position in Southern Italy was now vulnerable. The death of Roger II only accentuated the problem. A rebellion in Sicily ensued against Roger II's successor, William I, also known as William the Wicked. Fortunately for William the Wicked, he led a counter attack helping him to retake Bari. In 1185 to 1186, the Normans made a third grab at Byzantine territory. This time their invasions brought them close to Constantinople. Thessalonica, the Byzantine's second city, was sacked. Not long after, the Byzantines under Alexios Branas obtained a crucial victory against the Normans during the Battle of Demetritzes, ending with Byzantium reclaiming Thessalonica. Though the second city was reclaimed, the Normans did not go away empty-handed. The County Palatine of Kefalonia and Zakynthos (Ionian islands) were added to the Kingdom of Sicily.

The Norman Conquest

What the Normans are best known for are the Battle of Hastings, William the Conqueror, and their conquest in England.

WILLIAM THE CONQUEROR

After his death, William the Conqueror was given this title. During the 11th century, he was known as William the Bastard, because he was the illegitimate son of Robert the Magnificent. This state of affairs made it difficult for him to succeed his father as Duke of Normandy.

William became the new Duke of Normandy but he was far too young to rule. Almost immediately Norman knights turned on each and started more than a decade of violence as they grabbed land and power for themselves. They built castles and challenged authority, making the duchy like other regions of France. Senior lords ruling Normandy on behalf of William were killed in battle or simply murdered. The new guardians who took their places may well have been the murderers (Fordham, M., 2017).

Fortunately, the then-king of the Franks, Henry I, and his great-uncle, the archbishop Robert, backed William's ascent to the throne. In 1030, William became Duke of Normandy. As Rollo's great-great-great-grandson, William continued to brutally quell any form of rebellion as well as any mention of his illegitimacy or insult to his mother or her family (Cohen, 2018). Until 1047, Norman nobles fought relentlessly to overthrow William of Normandy, but his violent suppression of the rebellions cemented his position as Duke. Owing to his difficult ascent to the throne, William became cautious of advisors and remained extra vigilant about who he trusted. In 1050, he arranged a marriage with his first cousin, Mathilde of Flanders, further establishing himself as the Duke of Normandy.

THE SUCCESSION CRISIS

Things in Britain took a terrible turn for the Anglo-Saxon kings in 1066. Edward the Confessor of Wessex died that year. The problem was Edward the Confessor had borne no children, therefore, he had no heirs to the throne. With no direct successors, there were four principle claims to the throne: Edward Ætheling, Earl Harold Godwinson, Harald Hardrada, and William Duke of Normandy. According to the Norman perspective, King Edward, whose mother was of Norman lineage, named William as his successor in 1051. At the time, Harold Godwinson swore an oath in Normandy on King Edward's request, vowing to support William's ascension. There were four people present at King Edward's deathbed, one being Harold. King Edward's dying words were ambiguous, implying either that he wished for Harold to take the throne or for Harold to ensure William's succession. Despite Edward's vague last words, William 'believed' that an alleged oath sworn 15 years earlier took precedent, making him Edward's successor. What we know is that Harold Godwinson took to the throne and that Harald Hardrada allied with Tostig Godwinson to make his own vie for the throne. Harold Godwinson successfully overcame the alliance at the Battle of Stamford Bridge, but three weeks later William had come to make his claim.

THE BATTLE OF HASTINGS

On October 14th, 1066, one of the most memorable medieval battles took place. The Battle of Hastings, also referred to as the Battle of England, saw the army of William the Conqueror come up against the army of Harold Godwinson. The Norman army had been delayed by terrible conditions at sea, causing William the Conqueror to invade much later than planned. All in all, it took William nine months to plan his attack, obtaining military support from Flanders and the Duchy of Brittany.

Three weeks after the Battle of Stamford Bridge, Harold Godwinson encountered his new rival to the throne, William the Conqueror. Whether it had been due to carelessness on Harold's part or inspired by the plan to make a surprise attack on the Norman forces, the English forces had not all managed to assemble near Hastings, a seaside town in Sussex. The scattered English army could have been a key factor in why Harold Godwinson lost the battle. On the part of the Normans, there was no need to be hasty. William was still establishing his forces when Harold's army attacked, making the case for Harold hoping to catch the Normans by surprise. Harold's plan failed. Norman scouts spotted their attack, giving time for the Normans to respond effectively.

The English army consisted almost entirely of infantry. On the other hand, infantry, cavalry, and archers made up the Norman ranks. For the ranged soldiers, they opened the battle sending arrows into a shield war of infantry. The infantry held strong. Even though we have seen that the Norman chevaliers were infinitely deadlier in attack, in this case, the English infantry proved themselves capable of defending themselves. Whatever the Normans tried seemed to have little effect against the infantry. Historians are now torn on what followed.

During the early afternoon, the battle seemed to end in a stalemate. Soon, the Normans retreated. Here is where historians are torn. Most agree it was a feigned retreat, that the Normans regularly employed this tactic to thin out their opponent's lines. This is exactly what happened. The English went on the offense, but thinning lines against archers and cavalry was not a good idea. The range of the archers helped to weaken the lines further while the cavalry could charge at a speed.

Atamus of Montecassino recounts what happened next. Late in the battle, Harold Godwinson died after taking an arrow in the eye. The leaderless English army now lost all formation; some fled the scene. The Normans won the crucial battle at Hastings. We do not have the exact figures of how many soldiers participated in the battle. There are estimates that 2000 Norman lives were spent while 4000 English lost their lives.

Norman Rule

It took two more months after his victory in the Battle of Hastings for William of Normandy to be crowned King of England. From Sussex to London, the Norman Duke met English resistance. Moreover, Edward Ætheling—one of the four who had claims to the throne—was supported by important figures during the time such as Stigand, the archbishop of Canterbury, and the Bishop of York. It was these English forces who delayed William from being crowned king. Eventually, William the Conqueror was crowned king of England on December 25th, 1066.

Under Norman Rule, there were a number of changes, as to be expected, in England. With the Norman expansion, castles built in the Norman style—ringworks and Motte-and-Bailey castles—became commonplace. In total, 741 motte-and-bailey castles were built in England and Wales during Norman Rule. Though cavalry were not initially pivotal at the Battle of Hastings, they proved to be in the remainder of the Norman Conquest. As the Norman cavalry invaded England, they had the upper hand against the English, allowing the Normans to conquer the island. This tradition of Norman knights proved to be a fortunate contributor to William the Conqueror's campaign. He simply inherited an excellent military strategy, resulting in the Medieval historian, John Gillingham, referring to the Norman leader as "William the Lucky Bastard."

LANGUAGE AND CLASS

The Normans not only played an influential role in European history but also shaped contemporary society, mostly through language—and in this case, modern English. For most of us, Old English or Anglo-Saxon would be hardly comprehensible. An excellent example is the epic poem *Beowulf.* Since the Norman Conquest, significant changes such as the Great Vowel Shift were made to the English language, which is now known as Middle English or Anglo-Norman. Though the English which followed was Early Modern English—like that of Shakespeare—it is much more comprehensible thanks to the Norman influence on Anglo-Saxon. That is why we can still learn and read Shakespeare 500 years later.

Such a transition came at a cost. William the Conqueror did not speak any English. In official contexts like during legal proceedings only French was used. The consequence was Franglais (a hybrid of English and French). Contemporary English owes much to William the Conqueror as many words are borrowed—or stolen, depending on how you see it—from French.

CHAPTER TEN

HOLY ROMAN EMPIRE

C. 962–1806 CE

C harlemagne's reign was the precursor to the Holy Roman Empire. It was this pious inauguration proclaimed by Pope Leo III and seemingly ordained by God that gave rise to the concept of a holy empire.

We will cover the rise of the Holy Roman Empire and its gradual and long-lasting decay. The Holy Roman Empire was massive. In fact, it was more of a conglomerate of states, duchies, and regions. From its beginnings, it sought to emulate the dominance of the Roman Empire.

Rise From the Ashes

The Carolingian Empire disintegrated quickly. Charlemagne's grandsons split the empire, creating three kingdoms. The grandsons Charles, Lothair, and Louis decided that the ruler of the Middle Kingdom would be recognized as the true emperor. Under Lothair's reign, this kingdom was composed of Burgundy and Italy. It was in this kingdom specifically that relations quickly worsened, culminating in the creation of separate kingdoms of Burgundy and Italy.

Meanwhile in East Francia, after their King Conrad I died, the Frankish and Saxon nobles elected Henry the Fowler, the Duke of

Saxony, as the next king. When he died in 936, his eldest son Otto I, or Otto the Great, inherited his titles as King of Germany and Duke of Saxony. The other dukes of Bavaria, Swabia, Franconia, and Lorraine attended Otto I's coronation, swore fealty to the new king. Only a year later, Eberhard, the new duke of Bavaria, orchestrated a rebellion. Otto quelled the uprising, holding onto his reign.

During Eberhard's second attempt at rebellion, he and Otto met at the Battle of Andernach, for which Otto had recruited the assistance of the Dukes of Swabia and Alsace. Though the Archbishop attempted to negotiate peace between the parties, Otto preferred the peace-through-battle approach. At the Battle of Andernach, Eberhard was killed. For the next decade, 941 to 951, Otto consolidated power in East Francia—modern-day Germany.

After the king of Italy, Lothair II died, a rival, Berengar II seized the throne. In an attempt to legitimise his position, he betrothed his son to Lothair's widow Adelaide. She refused, was imprisoned, escaped, and sought the protection of Otto. When they married in September 951, Otto lay claim to Italy. Liudolf, Otto's son, led the invasion of Lombardy. Yet, he was unsuccessful, leaving Otto little choice but to come to his aid. Berengar, fled the capital Pavia, and Otto was handed the Iron Crown of the Lombards.

August 955 saw a defining moment for Otto as he defeated the Magyars at the Battle of Lechfeld. They were not just defeated, but annihilated, ending all Magyar threat to Western Europe indefinitely. With Otto's victory over the Magyars, the German army recognized Otto I as father of the fatherland and their emperor.

In 957, Liudolf died. As Otto had lost his army's commander, Berengar used weakness to attack the March (meaning frontier district) of Verona—which Otto had previously stripped Berengar of—and the Papal states. The Pope, John XII, sought aid from Otto. Feeling inspired by his success against the Magyars, his army's support, his marriage to Adelaide securing his title as king of Italy, and his success at converting the Magyars and other Slavs to Christianity, Otto took advantage of the pope's plea for help, using it as a bargaining chip to be crowned emperor. In February 962, Otto the Great's wish was granted. Pope John XII crowned him emperor, and his wife Adelaide empress of the Holy Roman Empire. The head of the Empire was transferred from the

Middle Kingdom to East Francia. Naturally, this move cast doubt on whether Charlemagne was the first Holy Roman Emperor.

Protection from Berengar's forces was not the only motivation behind Otto's coronation. Towards the end of the 9th century, the Magyars became a constant menace to Western Europe, particularly Germany. With this band of people—pagans—now in check, Otto was seen, like Charlemagne, as the savior of Christendom. In addition, he inspired a so-called Ottonian Renaissance where the empire reinvigorated its Roman roots. Following Byzantine tradition, libraries were built, Ottonian monasteries produced numerous illuminated texts—which contained miniature illustrations or borders— books were saved, and the arts experienced a revival. Key art pieces from this period include metalwork, the jeweled Crosses of Lothair, wall paintings, and portraits of rulers. A new hybrid of art was developed mixing elements of late antiquity with Byzantine and Carolingian culture.

The Four Phases of the Empire

AGE OF EMPERORS (962–1250)

After Otto I was crowned the Holy Roman Emperor, two significant consequences followed. The first phase of the Empire, the Age of Emperors, had begun. Next, instead of French, the king was now German. German royalty and aristocracy would hold the title until the empire's decline. Since Otto's inauguration, three aristocratic families ruled the kingdom: the Ottonian, Salian, and Supplinburg dynasties. In the shadow of the emperor's rule a new dynasty, specifically in Swabia, was gaining power. The Hohenstaufen (also Staufer) family were rising up the ranks. Through key arranged marriages and holding important offices, the family with Frederick I in 1079, was appointed Duke of Swabia by the then Salian king, Henry IV.

It is not known whether Henry IV's son, Henry V, played a role in deposing his father to ensure he succeeded him before claims were made on the crown. What we know is that in December 1105, Henry IV was forced to abdicate and hand over the crown. Though Henry V's coronation took place in February 1111, he started acting in an imperial role in 1106. Henry V died without any heirs. Fredrick II and Conrad III were both in line for the throne but the Supplinburg leader, Lothair of Supplinburg, was elected as king. On the mother's side, Agnes of Germany, Fredrick and Conrad were both grandsons to Henry IV. With their rightful succession denied, civil war ensued, starting in 1134 and ending in 1137, with the death of Lothair. Conrad III was elected king.

BARBAROSSA

Inheriting the Duchy of Swabia, Frederick I Barbarossa (1) participated in the second crusade where he obtained a wealth of military knowledge. His uncle, Conrad III, and the only other attendant, the prince-Bishop of Bamberg, testified that the king named Frederick his successor and not the king's son, also called Frederick IV of Hohenstaufen.

In 1152, Frederick was elected king by the princely electors. One of the key motivations for the princes to elect Frederick was they saw him as a figure who could unify the empire once more. It was not only the civil war in 1134 that had divided the empire, but an even worse one had plagued it for 50 years. During the reign of Henry IV, a power struggle ensued between him and Pope Gregory VII around whether the Papacy or the secular king had the right to elect archbishops. When the king refused this power to the papacy, they revolted against the crown. This division among the church and state occurred for 50 years and became known as the Investiture Controversy.

The struggle ended in 1122, but a rift marked the empire. It was this rift that Frederick's electors hoped to bridge. Related to the former king on his mother's side and to the king before that on his father's side, he could overcome the division between the Hohenstaufen and Guelphs. He took on the role of appointing officers from both families, known as *Minstrales*, to foster amiable relations.

ITALIAN CAMPAIGNS

Soon after taking office, Frederick—Barbarossa—left for Italy. Trade and population size made the wealth of Italy's northern cities attractive as a possible avenue to bring prosperity back to Germany. One might want to highlight an interesting detail connected with Frederick and his time in Italy. Barbarossa is well-known in German popular culture (2). Yet he is almost universally known by the Italian name *Barbarossa*—translating directly to Red Beard—instead of his German one *Kaiser Rotbart*, implying that Barbarossa will always be associated with his Italian campaigns.

In total, Barbarossa led six campaigns in Italy. First, in 1154, he planned an attack against the Norman king William I of Sicily. Making such a move first entailed marching through the peninsula, in which Frederick I encountered much resistance. After successfully besieging the Northern cities such as Milan, Pavia, and Tortona, in the Lombard capital, Pavia, he was crowned king of Italy, receiving the iron crown on April 24th. His conquest took him further inland, passing through the regions of Emilia-Romagna and Tuscany. He eventually came into sight of Rome. Pope Adrian IV had problems of his own then, struggling with hostile forces led by Arnold of Brescia. Barbarossa intervened. Arnold was hanged for treason to the dismay and anger of the Roman citizens. The pope crowned Barbarossa Holy Roman Emperor on June 18th despite the uproar of the Romans.

Dissent and division among the population occurred later in the peninsula. This time it was not confined to Rome but spread throughout the Papal, Lombard, and Holy Roman regions. In 1160, there was a dispute between Antipope Victor IV and Alexander III—a direct consequence of the East-West Schism occurring in Europe at the time. Barbarossa took Antipope Victor IV's side but also hoped to overcome the division. Owing to this schism, many Italian cities supported the Lombards, preventing him from achieving his initial goal. During Barbarossa's fifth campaign, he suffered his most devastating and personal loss. Frederick expected to be bolstered by his Guelph cousin, Henry the Lion, Duke of Bavaria and Saxony. But his cousin abandoned him moments before battle. In May 1176, it was at the Battle of Legnano (3) which halted Barbarossa's campaigns in Italy. Frederick was injured in the battle and incorrect reports of him being dead spread throughout the continent. These reports also spread news of his failure. Europeans were shocked to learn the Holy Roman Emperor had been defeated.

Following this humiliating and costly defeat, Barbarossa attempted to take a more diplomatic approach afterwards, including negotiating with the Lombards and relinquishing rule over Northern Italy. All in all, he managed to annex some parts of Tuscany and hang on to them, while also orchestrating advantageous marriages in Sicily through his children. Still keeping an eye on Italy, Barbarossa returned to Germany. Investment in Italy during his campaigns meant neglect on the home front. Feuds and opposition rose among noble families in Germany, but Frederick used this to his advantage to implement imperial law over traditional law. With this power, he stripped his treacherous cousin, Henry the Lion, of Saxony and Bavaria. As a Duke, Henry was a powerful figure, but Frederick took advantage of weakness in Germany to seize his lands and exile him. Once Henry was removed, Saxony and Bavaria lost their sovereignty.

ORIGINS OF THE EMPIRE'S NAME

It was two years after being crowned Emperor that Barbarossa started using the term *sacrum imperium*, meaning Holy Empire. Previously, Charlemagne was recognized as the new 'Roman' emperor, but thanks to Barbarossa's insistence on using this term, the empire is known as the Holy Roman Empire till today. Of course, there was plenty of motivation behind Barbarossa's reasons for calling it so, revealed in the following comment: "he believed himself to have been chosen by God to foster an institution that was the cornerstone of world order, the source of peace and justice" (Carson, T.E., 2002). A decade later saw the canonizing of Charlemagne as a saint, marking a deeper association with the empire and divinity.

FREDERICK II

It was during Barbarossa's grandson Frederick II's reign that the empire reached new heights, but ended abruptly for the Hohenstaufen dynasty. Born in Ancona (near Rome), Frederick was in line to rule the empire at the age of two, after his father Henry VI died at 32. For some years, his mother, Empress Constance, acted as his queen regent, but her death in 1198 forced a new succession crisis. Even by medieval standards, four years old was too young to rule a kingdom. Empress Constance left Pope Innocent III as Frederick's guardian. Though her choice was made partly owing to her Catholic background, this was mostly a political move. By putting Frederick's guardianship under the pope's authority, years later it could not be overturned. For his part, Innocent III could not stop an ambitious German lord, Markward, from making claims to Italian territory—namely Sicily—but the pope was effective in organizing an advantageous marriage for Frederick to the Spanish princess, Constance of Aragon. Fortunately, Markward died some years later.

Frederick's marriage to Constance of Aragon allowed him access to a rather large army, even though his wife was 16 years his senior. The age gap proved to be another stroke of fortune for Frederick, as his wife became his political advisor. A year before his marriage in 1209, Frederick ended the pope's guardianship, seeking to take the helm of the Holy Roman Empire which was, after all, his birthright. Meanwhile in Germany, a follower of Richard the Lionheart, namely Otto of Brunswick had other plans. Frederick's uncle Philip of Swabia was crowned the new king of Germany. Otto of Brunswick had intended to marry Philip of Swabia's daughter but was rejected. The German lord responded by murdering the German king. The pope realized that if Frederick ceded power in Germany, it would not be long until the Italian peninsula became the new target of attacks. So, to separate Sicily from the kingdom in the North, he sided with Otto of Brunswick.

After Otto IV was crowned Holy Roman Emperor by the pope in 1209, and as predicted, the Italian peninsula drew the new emperor's eye. However, Otto IV continued on to Sicily, leaving Pope Innocent III little choice but to support Frederick's claims as emperor. As it was the pope's power to coronate emperors, he could technically 'uncoronate' them, which he did. In 1210, the pope excommunicated him. As we had learned from Barbarossa's campaigns in Italy, which were an attempt to restore German wealth, the opposite occurred. The more time Otto spent abroad in Italy, the more the princes and lords of duchies of Francia garnered power. Internal conflict within the states was making the overall empire weaker. Otto's campaign in Italy, unlike Barbarossa's, was not supported by the German nobility. The Danish King Valdemar II had been making attacks on Germany at the time, and the German aristocrats felt Otto was leaving their duchies defenseless by being in

Italy engaged in pope fights. Thus, when Otto was excommunicated, his ambitions in Italy halted soon after.

With Otto out of the way, Innocent III planned to subdue Frederick II by distracting him with the sixth crusade. Since every other crusade had failed, Frederick did not especially covet the idea of embarking on the sixth one. Furthermore, the shameful fall and sacking of Constantinople in 1198—covered in chapter 5—was still a very recent and unpleasant reminder of the internal hostility in Europe. So though Innocent III's plan was to send Frederick II to Jerusalem, the latter remained in Sicily where he rebuilt the kingdom. The restoration of Sicily was completely necessary. Frederick II's father, Henry VI, had come to Sicily with a similar plan to Barbarossa—to plunder the kingdom and redirect its wealth to Germany. Apart from that, royal officers and noble lords had resorted to backbiting politics, where individuals often betrayed one another. More so, the rise of Genoa in the Tyrrhenian Sea meant that Sicily's own coffers were slowly diminishing.

Knowing what we already know of Sicily's medieval history, the island had been under the rule of Byzantines, Lombards, Normans, and Arabs. It was partly due to this ethnic split which caused the increased levels of lawlessness and violence in Sicily. Frederick, raised in Sicily, was fluent in Arabic, French, German, Greek, Latin, and Sicilian, making him the perfect person to bring about cultural and ethnic harmony. Under his authority, Jews were protected. Even though there had been five crusades prior to his rule, Frederick recruited Arabs as well as Christians into his bodyguard, but also sent many Arabs and Muslims to work as blacksmiths in Apulia.

The Sixth Crusade

Every Crusade failed except Frederick's. While buying time in Sicily, an opportune marriage to Isabella II of Jerusalem appeared in 1225. As she was the heiress to Jerusalem, Frederick's marriage to Isabella II now gave him the motivation to embark on the Sixth Crusade. Except that during August 1227, when he did set out, he succumbed to illness, forcing him to return to Italy and separate with his army who were on their way to Jerusalem. Pope Innocent III believed this was a sign of betrayal by Frederick II so he excommunicated him.

This sort of placed Frederick II in a kind of twilight zone. He was excommunicated and could not rule, but he could not undo his excommunication by going on the crusade because excommunication forbade him from doing so. The only way to undo his excommunication was by handing over the kingdom of Sicily to the papacy. Marriage to Isabella II guaranteed Jerusalem to Frederick II so he left anyway, handing Sicily to the pope. As mentioned, the sixth crusade was the only one which saw Jerusalem being transferred to the Christians. This Frederick II achieved not by war, but by negotiation. History.com says, "In 1229, in what became known as the Sixth Crusade, Emperor Frederick II achieved the peaceful transfer of Jerusalem to Crusader control through negotiation with al-Kamil" (History.com Editors, 2020).

ITALY

Though the sixth crusade was the most successful of all the others and took the form of a negotiation more than a crusade, by 1244, a fresh Muslim offensive saw the city lost to the Muslims again. Fortunately, during Frederick II's time in Jerusalem, he enjoyed peaceful relations with the papacy. A new problem appeared in Germany. Frederick II's son, Henry VII, had implemented aggressive policies against the German princes who had steadily been increasing their power. What ensued was that the German princes limited Henry VII's power, naming through the policy *Statutum in favorem principum* (statues in favor of princes). Frederick signed another policy in Cividale agreeing to the princes' demands, asking his son to meet him in Aquileia in 1232. However, the League of Lombard was reestablished in Northern Italy where cities such as Brescia, Milan, and Bologna joined forces to revolt against Frederick II's rule. With his hands full in northern Italy, Henry went back to Germany and renewed his attempts to stop the princes in their tracks. Frederick II needed aid from the German princes for military support in northern Italy, leaving him little choice but to go to Germany, seize his son's lands, and imprison him. Using the princes' backing, Frederick II returned to Italy with an army.

Two specific factions, the Guelphs and Ghibellines, have become ingrained in history for the infamous Guelphs and Ghibelline Wars. The wars started from a feud originating during Barbarossa's Italian campaigns. As you will remember, the Guelphs were a royal German family which Barbarossa could overcome by being related to the Guelphs and Hohenstaufen. It was also Henry the Lion, his Guelph cousin, that betrayed him.

Well, the betrayal continued with the next generation. A faction of the royal family and adherents grew in Northern Italy, hoping to prevent Barbarossa from encroaching on more Lombard land. Obviously, the original feud rival appeared to support Barbarossa. Though known as the Hohenstaufen, in Northern Italy they were known as Ghibelline, which was an Italian translation of Waiblingen, a castle based in Southwest Germany. Over the course of the 13th and 14th centuries, these factions were at war. One of the most famous battles was the Battle of Cortenuova.

Pope Innocent took the side of the Lombard League. The last thing the papacy wanted was to be wedged between lands controlled by the Holy Roman Empire in the north and south. Frederick's intentions were to suppress the Lombard communes who supported the pope and failed to recognize Frederick as the Holy Roman Emperor.

Twice in a row the Lombard League was crushed, but during November 1237 they were incorrectly made to believe—by none other than the emperor himself—that he and his forces were staying at Cremona for the winter. The Lombards took the bait.

Their army marched across the Ogilo River for Cremona—except Frederick had scouts planted who cleverly used smoke signals to inform the Imperial Army of the approaching enemies. Once they crossed the river, they saw the smoke signals and the writing was on the wall. At Cortenuova (near Bergamo), they got into formation preparing for battle. The Lombard League was made of a conglomeration of Northern Italians and Guelphs, while on the Imperial side there was a confederation of Muslim archers from Apulia, Ghebelline, and Sicily. From the moment the battle began, it went in favor of the imperial army. His horsemen penetrated the Lombardian defensive line, causing them to retreat. Fortunately, retreat into Cortenuova allowed them to protect themselves until the Muslim archers and Teutonic Knights came upon the scene. A spell of luck came for the Lombard army. Reinforcements arrived from Bergamo and they immediately set about aiding further retreat of the Northern Italian confederation. Yet, the luck of the

Lombards expired the next day. After spending their night sleeping in their armor, Frederick's forces were expected to continue fighting at daybreak, but the Lombards could no longer resist the Imperial forces.

The aftermath of the war saw the Lombard League completely annihilated. With nothing to stop Frederick from invading the Papal states, Frederick marched on this territory and as a result, Pope Gregory IX was excommunicated, and Frederick returned to Sicily waiting for the next papal election.

Four short years later, the Mongols turned their attention to Western Europe. After utterly devastating Hungary, Poland, and Romania, the Mongol military might brought them to Austria. After two failed Mongol attacks in Olomouc and Theben (both in Czech Republic), it seemed destined that a full-on invasion would occur. Frederick asked for assistance from England and France. Yet, he could breathe a sigh of relief since the Mongols never attacked the Holy Roman Empire.

LITERATURE, POLICY, AND RELIGION

One of the popular names of endearment that Frederick II has been called by is *stupor mundi*, Latin for "wonder of the world." From a Sicilian perspective, he was considered as much since he was the first of the German dynasty to invest in this kingdom, as opposed to sacking for all its worth and making away with all its wealth. In fact, Frederick II was mostly uninterested in Germany, having further consequences which we will see in the next section. When any pope excommunicated him, nothing pleased him more because it meant he could live in Sicily. He took an avid interest in hunting with birds of prey. *De arte venandi cum avibus* is a collection of six books on the "The Art of Hunting With Birds" written by Frederick during the 13th century. While there were innovations taking place in Byzantium, the Arabian World, and other parts of Europe, Frederick II focused on literature, specifically poetry. He is credited with creating the 14-line sonnet for which Shakespeare and other Elizabethan writers would adapt.

Finally, several popes had excommunicated Frederick including Pope Gregory IX's successor, Pope Innocent IV. There has been some speculation about Frederick II being atheist, but other historians have mentioned that this was not the case, rather that Frederick was skeptical about the papacy. It did not help matters that Pope Innocent IV renewed the crusade against Frederick to have him deposed as emperor, once again excommunicating him and calling him *preambulus Antichristi* (the predecessor of the Antichrist), which was just about the harshest declaration for the time. Parma, a Lombard city, managed to oust the Imperial forces, leading to a series of events. Pockets of rebels started targeting Imperial communes and cities such as Romagne, Marche, and Spoleto. Frederick's forces could not overcome these losses and these territories were lost. The loss of Parma in February 1248 to the Lombards had proven even more significant, as the Imperial treasure was kept there and now in the hands of Lombard enemies. After the Battle of Parma in February 1248, where Frederick unsuccessfully tried to place Parma back under Imperial control, it ended with the emperor's defeat, and he fled to Sicily where he lived until 1250.

AGE OF PRINCES (1250–1415)

When Frederick II met his death, his line ended and the empire entered a period known as the Great *Interregnum* where the empire experienced its longest time without an emperor. This period was characterized by continuous contests between various dynasties, most notably the Hohenstaufen and anti-Hohenstaufen factions such as the Guelphs. When Frederick II died, there were two possible heirs: Frederick's son Conrad IV and William of Holland. In 1254, Conrad IV died. Two years later, William died. The next year, an election was held. Richard of Cornwall and Alfonso of Castile both won. Four of the seven German princes (4) and Richard was crowned as King of Germany. However, in 1272 he met his death. By 1272, the empire had been further broken down into smaller dynasties who all managed to seize more and more territory. Two specifically powerful figures appeared: Ottokar II of Bohemia and Rudolf of Habsburg. Rudolf of Habsburg was elected as king, becoming the first Habsburg to do so, but like Richard he was never crowned emperor. The Habsburg family would gain more and more power over claiming territories previously owned by the Hohenstaufen, as the former dynasty had gone through financial troubles and sold them to the latter dynasty. With the family's wealth and territory established, his authority among the German princes grew until he was elected. For more than the next century, the princes continued to hold true dominance in the empire as it was only who won the election who could be crowned as king. During this age, the princes kept a careful eye on the Habsburg family, electing, for example, Henry of Luxembourg, simply to prevent dominance of the Habsburgs.

THE EARLY HABSBURG PERIOD (1415–1555)

There are so many eccentricities, tragedies, and scandals involving the Habsburgs or Habsburg dynasty that it is impossible to cover them all. Probably the most famous is the assassination of Franz Ferdinand starting the First World War. There is also family inbreeding, the War of the Spanish Succession, the rebellion of the legendary William Tell, and the Defenestration of Prague—where Protestants threw Catholic authorities out of windows to protest against Habsburg rule. While the Habsburg family were undeniably eccentric, the reason for so many scandals is that the dynasty endured so long, originating in 1020 until the present day. During that time, they ruled over the Holy Roman Empire, Switzerland, and Austria-Hungary. It is impossible to cover the entire history of such an interesting family.

In what is modern-day Switzerland, Otto II took over a castle named Habichtsburg giving rise to the name Habsburg. Otto II is considered one of the founding members of the Habsburg family. During the 12th century, they developed close relations with the Hohenstaufens allowing them to easily take over territory as well as hold official positions in the kingdom. For instance, the count Werner II—Rudolf I's great-great grandfather—fought for Barbarossa at the Battle of Monte Porzio where he died. Another instance was when Rudolf II, in 1198, funded Frederick's war and joined the war alongside the Ghibelline forces, supporting the Hohenstaufen family. As a result, the emperor became godfather to Rudolf I who would become the German king in the next century. During these early days, the family signaled their route to power, preferring to use diplomacy as opposed to military force to get ahead. One especially powerful tool that the Habsburgs relied on was marriage, used for advantageous alliances. The expression *Bella gerant alii, tu felix Austria nube*, which translates to "Others wage war, you Fortunate Austria, marry," clearly indicates the Habsburg habit.

There were some significant factors which allowed Rudolf I to become the German king. On his father's deathbed, he inherited the title of count from his father. An advantageous marriage led to annexation of important territories, a maternal uncle's death and extinction of the bloodline meant Rudolf absorbed even more valuable territories, and finally, close friendships with Frederick II and King Conrad IV of Germany included rewards of even more land. As soon as Rudolf became the most powerful prince in the empire, opportunities for powerful alliances through marriage appeared such as Rudolf's two daughters' betrothals to Albert II, Duke of Saxony, and Louis II, Duke of Upper Bavaria and Palatine.

As we have already seen, the princes' held true power from the second half of the 13th century, but in 1273, seven of the princes had voted for Rudolf as king of Germany. Though there was some opposition during the election, the Habsburg family proved the utility in advantageous unions. Interestingly, the decision to elect Rudolf king as opposed to other choices at the time came from the princes hoping to hang on to their own power for much longer. Rudolf was 55 years old. They did not expect a long reign. However, the very next year, Rudolf began his tenure with great fervor. At the Imperial Diet—a forum used for negotiations between princes and the ecclesiastical body —Rudolf decreed that all land seized after Frederick II's death had to be restored. Ottokar, who also had opposed Rudolf's coronation, openly defied such a move. Both camps, Ottokar and Rudolf, made alliances and the two went to war in 1278 at the Battle of the Marchfeld in what is modern-day lower Austria. Victory went to Rudolf and Ottokar was killed. Rudolf annexed Ottokar's territories, which covered much of what is Austria in the present-day. In 1291, after a 17-year reign, Rudolf died. His son, Albert I, inherited his title, but was assassinated by Duke John—aptly known as John Parricida. After the Treaty of Rheinfelden forced him to relinquish his duchies, he believed that Albert I had stolen his inheritance. Luck had seemingly run out for the Habsburgs. Frederick III or Frederick the Fair was not elected as king.

In 1437, the last of male member of the House of Luxembourg died. Before the event took place, Albert II of Germany, a Habsburg, had not only inherited a number of territories as his father was the Duke of Austria and his mother affiliated with Bavaria, but also initiated a couple of advantageous marriages—one to Elizabeth of Luxembourg and the other to Barbara of Celje in what is now Slovenia—putting a large amount of territory at his disposal.

After the short reign of Sigismund, as his successor, Albert was crowned king of Hungary as well as king of Bohemia. The Bohemian king could never truly rule over Bohemia, as the citizens and Polish were engaged in a conflict preventing him from doing so. Despite being elected "King of the Romans," Albert was not crowned the emperor. It seems that this was a title that Albert was not interested in. It was only a decade after Albert's death that the first Habsburg was crowned Holy Roman Emperor. In 1452, Frederic III became the fourth Holy Roman Emperor. From this time onwards, the Habsburgs would hold the title for the next century until the empire's dissolution.

FEUDALISM

Even before Habsburg reign, several changes allowed their continued leadership beyond the medieval period. From the chapter on the Venetian republic, we learned how the lack of land promoted independence, mercantilism, banking, and more advanced forms of capitalism. Almost the opposite was true in the Holy Roman Empire, where land served as the most basic currency. Over-importance of land led to a complex system of feudalism in the Holy Roman Empire—almost a form of hyper-feudalism. Like we saw in France, the various duchies or vassals owned territory which they awarded to noble families in exchange for payment and military support. A similar system occurred in this empire, except that there were various types of agreements between the vassals and lords, duchies and princes, and even the ecclesiastical body. While it is impossible to cover the nature of all the different agreements, some examples include *Afterlehen* and *Burglehn*. The former allowed a fiefdom to be divided further into a subfief while the latter allowed a vassal to give a lord or governor (*burgmannnen*) a castle and/or the surrounding area of a castle in exchange for payment and services. Though the Holy Roman Empire was ruled by the Habsburgs, its impossibly complex feudal system watered down the power they truly had.

It was not until the 13th century that the rise of cities gave the Holy Roman Emperors more power. Cities meant less importance was placed on territory. Aristocratic feudalism was on the decline as cities and nation-states started to form. Wealth was less concentrated among nobles. And the Holy Roman Emperor would do more to encourage this by granting more positions of office to Bourgeoise members, where previously landowners would generally qualify for these roles. The more developed and central an area, the more rapidly this process of nation-building would occur. In more outer-lying areas, feudal practices were maintained but would slowly disappear over time, too. In the 12th century, the appearance of guilds protecting classes of workers and merchants emerged, signifying the beginnings of a move away from feudalism. The rise of mercantilism allowed the Holy Roman Empire to dominate trade, increasing the empire's wealth. As the majority of merchants were established in cities, they were under the legal system of the ruler. That being said, there were several cities, called Free Imperial Cities, that evaded control from their respective governors including Basel, Cologne, and Strasbourg.

Reformation and Nation State

During the Imperial Diets from 1434 to 1438, Sigismund and the prince-electors attempted to introduce reform. Both intended to make the empire run more efficiently, except they were hoping for more power in their hands. Several changes were made including banning feuds, making provisions for rights on coinage (who legally could essentially mint coins), and other administrative functions. Imperial forces made decisions on these aspects, but the lack of similar vision by Sigismund and the prince-electors made it largely unsuccessful.

Under Maximilian I, at the end of the 15th century, Imperial Reform took place. Largely in response to financing the war against the Ottomans and the French in Italy, the imperial tax was raised. Naturally, some conditions had to be met before the statue could be implemented. These laid the foundations for Imperial Reform. First, Roman Law was enforced and became the legal system throughout Imperial territory. While there were lower courts which dealt with local cases and applied customary Germanic Law, it was reserved for lower courts. The next century saw a supreme court (*Reichskammergericht*) created for the entire empire. Feuds between lords and vassals did become outlawed through the passing of *Ewiger Landfriede*—Perpetual Peace—banning all forms of medieval vendettas. An Imperial Government was to be introduced which meant that the princes would have more power, but Maximilian still contested this and it was only in 1500 that he agreed.

Finally, Maximilian, as well as specific clerical figures, pushed the narrative of the nation-state, particularly the German one. An important cultural artifact was discovered, namely the Roman historian, Tactitus' *Germania*. Joachim Whaley, a professor of German history and thought at Cambridge, reveals how political quests such as the emphasis on a German nation-state formed a new political climate during Maximilian's reign. While it extends beyond the Middle Ages, such notions would begin to characterize the latter part of this millennium. Events such as the Second Schleswig War and Seven Weeks War were born centuries before.

THE FINAL PHASE (1555–1806)

Napoleon was not called Master of Europe by accident. Against Napoleon—considered the greatest general ever—the Austrians had little hope. Nonetheless, the Battle of Austerlitz (1805), where the French met the Austrians, is celebrated as Napoleon's decisive victory—a true testament of his military prowess. "The name of Austerlitz will forever be linked with that of Napoleon Bonaparte" (Adams, M., 2005). For the Holy Roman Empire, the pressure of continued defeat in battle and the political realities of the day, finally culminated on August 6, 1806, when Emperor Francis II abdicated the imperial title and dissolved the empire.

If there is any empire which is more complex and more perplexing, it would be the Holy Roman Empire. Interestingly, its deeply layered feudal system allowed it to endure. The Habsburgs' ability to negotiate and form alliances was achieved by their secret weapon, marriage, which ironically contributed to their decline. Why, you ask? Too many claimants to the throne. The more individuals you let into your bloodlines, the more claims there are to the throne. The Treaty of Westphalia was truly responsible for the empire's demise, but it limped right through the Renaissance until the Age of Enlightenment when the Master of Europe quickly ended their long years of dominion.

CHAPTER ELEVEN

THE GRAND DUCHY OF LITHUANIA

c. 1236-1569 CE

A s the last state to convert to Christianity, tucked away in the
northeast corner, a Baltic/Ruthenian nation emerged to become
the strongest confederation during the early 15th century. After a series
of unsuccessful crusades, bands of Baltic duchies banded together and
created a powerful Grand Duchy.

Origins and Geography

When learning about the Grand Duchy of Lithuania, it is crucial
to understand that initially the territory of this kingdom occupied
modern-day Belarus and Lithuania. Learning about this kingdom's
history involves studying part of Belarusian history. There was also a
Baltic nation called the Samogitians occupying the northwest corner of
present-day Lithuania, a territory named Žemaitija (Samogitia).

During the Great Migration period, there too was a migration
of Slavic peoples, the most notable was the Ruthenians. There is
still some controversy over whether the Ruthenians were Slavs or
Varangians—Viking Raiders. What we do know is that the state Rus, also

known as Kievan Rus, existed from the 9th to 13th century. Over years, Rus culture was composed of Slavic and Baltic culture, the most obvious marker being language.

It was on the legacy of the Ruthenians (Rus people) and Lithuanians that the Grand Duchy of Lithuania was formed. What we know for certain about these peoples, the Ruthenians and Samogitians, is that they were pagans. And it was their pagan following which spurred the creation of the Duchy.

Formations

Between 1180 and 1183, the band of Lithuanians (1) grew in strength so much so that they withstood attacks from the Principality of Polotsk, a thorn in the Lithuanian side during the 12th century. The tables soon turned. The Lithuanians began conducting their own raids on Polotsk, Pskov, and Novgorod, the latter two in Russia. With Lithuanian might increasing, this brought about a consolidation of Lithuanian territory, called Aukštaitija.

The Crusades did not end; destinations just changed. In 1208, Teutonic Knights and the Livonian Order began a series of crusades on the Lithuanians and Samogitians. These orders made it their mission to extend Christendom into the Baltic region. The Teutonic Order—also known as Teutonic Knights—were a religious group of German knights, established at the end of the 12th century. Originally they were merchants, but during the Crusades they changed their vocation and founded the Hospital of St. Mary of the German House in Jerusalem. A Teutonic Knight could be identified by his white habit with a black cross. After the Crusades failed, this religious order was given lands in Eastern Europe. As many people living in Eastern Europe were not Christian and occupied land close to Teutonic Knights, the latter soon took on the role of spreading Christianity to these parts. A particularly famous Teutonic Knight was Herman Balk, who became Master of Prussia. It was under Balk who took his men into Riga, placing other members of the order into castles and administrators of Livonia (now Latvia) under the authority of the bishop of Riga, establishing the Livonian Order, short for Livonian Brothers of the Sword.

After unsuccessful campaigns in Hungary, the Teutonic and Livonian orders turned their attention to the Lithuanians and Samogitians. The Livonians encouraged conflict in these parts to end raids in their territory. This military intervention backfired. All it did was unite these two nations under one ruler, Mindaugas, in 1253. Under the Treaty of Galicia-Volhynia, Žemaitija and Aukštaitija merged, with Žemaitija becoming one of the two administrative cores of the Grand Duchy.

In 1219, the Teutonic and Livonian Orders became the common enemies of all 21 duchies of Lithuania, thus necessitating the title Grand Duchy (*Magnus Ducatus Lithuania*). It should be noted that though the Teutonic and Livonian Orders posed the most pressing concern for the Duchies of Lithuania, they were not the only threat. Kievan Rus had fallen to the Mongols and fear of these hordes was spreading like wildfire through Eastern Europe. If they stood together, there was a better chance of survival.

The Grand Duchy Is Born

In total, there were 21 Lithuanian duchies. Under the conditions named by the Treaty of Galicia-Volhynia, five of them were held by senior dukes which were from Aukštaitija: Živinbudas, Daujotas, Vilikaila, Dausprungas, and Mindaugas. According to the *Livonian Rhymed Chronicle*, Mindaugas became the supreme ruler of the whole of Lithuania. Mindaugas' road to power is unclear. Some have stated that strategic marriages and murder of his rivals allowed for his ascent. After a defeat at the Battle of Saule in 1236, the Livonians' hopes to end Lithuanian raids were dashed. With the Livonians now vulnerable, Lithuania took advantage. The raids continued and Hrodna and Navahrudak—in Belarus—were annexed.

Twelve years later, civil war broke out. The Samogitians, under Vykintas, expressed open dissatisfaction against Mindaugas' supreme power and created a powerful coalition with the Livonians and other Lithuanian dukes. Demonstrating political cunning, Mindaugas exploited internal tension in the Baltic region and gained the Livonians as an ally. Promises the duke made included converting to Christianity and making Lithuania a Christian state.

In 1251, Mindaugas was baptized and Pope Innocent IV issued a decree announcing the Kingdom of Lithuania. Once the civil war ended, Mindaugas was crowned king in 1253. For 10 years, there was peace in which the king was preoccupied with expanding Lithuania's borders. Soon, rule extended from the upper Dvina River in the northeast to the Dnieper River in the southeast and the Pripet Marshes in the south. The king made a pivotal move which would have far-reaching consequences: He broke the alliance with the Livonians and renounced his faith. Interestingly, Mindaugas' nephew, the Grand Duke Treniota encouraged their king to do so, but he and Daumantas, the Prince of Pskov, assassinated Mindaugas and his two sons. Internal peace was shattered.

THE GEMINID DYNASTY

For the next seven years, the state of Lithuania was marked by internal fighting. At this stage there were several Grand Dukes. Traidenis, one of the grand dukes, came to power in 1269.

Under Traidenis' reign, Lithuania reverted to being a Pagan state. As the Livonian and Teutonic Orders had conquered the other Baltic tribes, the only Pagans who still remained were the Lithuanians. Both in 1270 and 1279, Lithuania, under Traidenis, successfully repelled the Orders. The duke also extended territory into Black Ruthenia (western Belarus).

VYTENIS

In 1295, Vytenis ascended to the throne. Under Vytenis, a centralized government was established. An early accomplishment made by Vytenis was forging an alliance with Riga. After swearing to protect them from the Livonians—and a vague promise to convert to Christianity—an alliance with Riga was won. Subsequently, the Livonians were defeated at the Battle of Turaida in 1298. This began Vytenis' 11 campaigns into Teutonic territory—one which saw a massacre at Brodnica (in modern-day Poland).

With the further expansion of their territories, the crucial alliance with Riga, and creating the strong centralized state, Vytenis is recognized as one of the greatest Grand Dukes. When he died in 1316, his two-decade reign ended.

GEDIMINAS

Like Vytenis, Gediminas is another key figure in Lithuanian history. There are claims that he was Vytenis' brother, cousin, and even his son. There were also rumors, probably started by the Teutonic Order, that Gediminas had killed Vytenis to usurp him. Gediminas established the Gediminid Dynasty and for the next century, this dynasty ruled the empire. On ascending to the throne, Gediminas inherited a vast territory consisting of Samogitia, Minsk, Podlasie, Polotsk, and Navahrudak, and Lithuania Proper.

In 1319, Gediminas chose Paganism, rejecting an alliance with the Livonian Order in favor of one with the Tartars. Despite this return to Paganism, the historian Aliksandr Kraukevic who specializes in Belarussian history, reveals that religious tolerance was present in the Great Duchy, especially to Catholic and Orthodox followers.

Gediminas took this religious tolerance much further, showing much temerity by successfully negotiating with the Pope John Paul XXII against Teutonic invasions. Not only did such Papal support stop the raids, but now Gediminas offered protection to noble figures and knights. In exchange for their labor as soil tillers, these new settlers built their own homesteads to be governed by their own choice of law.

While the relationship between the two entities remains unclear, it did not stop the Lithuanians from annexing previously conquered Mongolian territories, particularly those south and west of Kievan Rus. Once more, Lithuanian size expanded under Gediminas. The historian, Kraukevic, mentions this territorial expansion was largely thanks to Gediminas straightforward policy's, "defend in the West, attack in the East" (Astapenia, R., 2014) meaning the Grand Duchy increased threefold. Kraukevic summarizes Gediminas' successful 25-year rule over the Duchy, "Gedimin came to power in 1316 when the territory of the state was around 90,000 square kilometers. 25 years later he left the state with a territory of nearly 320,000 square kilometers" (Astapenia, R. 2014).

Olgerd and Kęstutis

Gediminas named his youngest son, Jaunutis, to be in possession of the capital, Vilnius, after his father's death. Jaunutis proved to be an unfit leader. His brothers, Olgerd (2) (also known as Algirdas) and Kęstutis, taking more active participation in the kingdom, successfully had him removed. In 1337, the position, Duchy of Trakai, was created as a kind of second-in-command position. After Jaunutis was deposed, Kęstutis received the Duchy of Trakai. From there onwards, the two brothers co-ruled harmoniously: Olgerd over the East and Kęstutis over the West.

During their reign, there was another concern: the Golden Horde. In 1333 and 1339 and later in the early 1360s, there were battles fought between the Mongols and Lithuanians (3). The most famous conflict between these peoples, fought either in 1362 or 1363, was the Battle of Blue Waters.

After the death of their leader, Berdi Beg Khan, the Golden Horde had fractured into smaller hordes known as *Ulus*. The Crimean *Ulus*, composed of Tartars, lacked any real cohesion without Khan. Exploiting their weakness, Olgerd initiated a series of campaigns into Kievan Rus annexing them from the Horde. These included Chernigov, Bryansk, Dykra, and Podolia. Now the Grand Duchy also had access to the Black Sea, their kingdom stretching from the Baltic to the Black Sea. We also see that the empire was extending further east into Dykra and Bryansk (now in Russia). Another significant contribution to the Grand Duchy during Olgerd's time was his marriage to Maria of Vitebsky, allowing the crucial Principality of Vitebsk to join the Grand Duchy.

Polish–Lithuanian Union

Up until the late 14th century, Poland remained a staunch ally with Hungary. However, a succession crisis in Poland occurred when King Casimir died in 1370, leaving no male heirs. His Hungarian nephew, Louis of Anjou, thus became king of Hungary and Poland, but also died in 1380. The succession would then be passed down to Louis' daughters, Mary and Jadwiga (also Hedwig). Mary married the future Holy Roman Emperor, Sigismund of Luxembourg after he invaded Slovakia (then a part of the Hungarian Kingdom), forcing Mary to marry him. Before these events happened, the Polish rejected Mary as their monarch and named Jadwiga—who was 10 years old—as their monarch. One theory is that Jadwiga was chosen by the Polish lords because she was young, so she could be easily manipulated.

Jadwiga had been previously promised to William of Austria, a Habsburg. The Polish Lords were especially worried about such a union so they contrived for it not to happen. The history is a bit sketchy here. Either the union and consummation did not occur and William was literally locked out of the castle, or it happened and he was removed afterwards.

What followed was the Grand Duke of Lithuania, Jogaila—a descendant of Olgerd— proposed to Jadwiga. For the Polish Lords, there was something to be gained from the union. First, it meant a possible return of the fertile lands of Galicia-Volhynia. Second, it meant Lithuania would no longer be a threat. For Lithuania, marriage to Sofia of the Grand Duchy of Moscow would not be advantageous because it would not prevent the continuous crusades of the Teutonic and Livonian Orders. The dominant or state religion of Moscow was Orthodoxy and, after the East-West Schism, the archenemy of Catholicism. If Jogalia married Sofia of Moscow, he could not neutralize the Teutonic Knights. There was one major concession—Lithuania had to be Christianised under Catholicism.

After Jadwiga's mother accepted Jogaila's proposal, Jogalia was baptized in Kraków on February 15th, 1386, and was referred to as Władysław II Jagiełło. Three days later, he married Jadwiga and they co-ruled over both Poland and the Grand Duchy of Lithuania.

Though there was a union now between Poland and Lithuania, both countries had their own currencies and laws, and, before a year ago, different religious beliefs. Nonetheless, as mentioned, the alliance was built on convenience—protecting themselves from other aggressive neighbors.

Vytautas

When Jagiełło became King of Poland, in his place he named his brother, Skirgaila, as his regent. Skirgaila was unpopular with the Lithuanians. Jagiełło's cousin, Vytautas, contested for the position of king regent. Yet, for many years, Jagiełło was reluctant to side with Vytautas.

When Vytautus was named the regent, he renewed the conquest east. He aided Tokhtamysh, the Khan of the Golden Horde, to regain power and was rewarded with more land. In 1398, Vytautas attacked Crimea, extending the Duchy's control near the Black Sea. During these last years of the 14th century, Vytautus named himself *Supremus Dux Lithuaniae* (the supreme duke of Lithuania). Finally, as part of his land extension program, Vytautas signed a treaty with the Duchy's natural enemy, the Teutonic Order, giving up Žemaitija (Samogitia) in exchange for Pskov and Novogod. The *Supremus Dux Lithuaniae* ruled the Duchy until 1430.

THE BATTLE OF GRUNWALD

The causes of this memorable battle occurred over two centuries. The Teutonic and Livonian Order had been engaged in Crusades against the Lithuanians to convert these pagans to Catholicism. Yet all motivation should have ceased after almost all of the Duchy converted, except one region: Žemaitija. More importantly, Žemaitija separated the Livonian Order from the Teutonic Order and gave the Lithuanian Duchy access to the Baltic Sea.

To help him secure his position as regency, Vytautas formed a provisional alliance with the Livonian Order, handing over Žemaitija to them in 1390 with the Treaty of Königsberg (now Kaliningrad). Two years later, Jagiełło named Vytautas his king regent. At the time, discontent was growing in Poland about Jagiełło diverting too much interest to Lithuanian issues instead of Polish ones. And Poland certainly had their own issues. Before Jagiełło had married Jadwiga, a war from 1326 to 1333 with the Teutonic Order entailed Poland losing its only access to the Baltic Sea.

Yet in 1409, after relinquishing Žemaitija to the Orders, the Samogitians rejected Christian baptisms and started their second rebellion. The Duchy, using rivers as networks, sent supplies to the Samogitians and now with war looming, Poland had to declare support for Lithuania or not. In 1409, they aligned themselves with the Lithuanians. Wenceslaus, King of the Holy Roman Empire, mediated and brought the three nations to sign a truce, expiring in July the following year. All the treaty did was buy the nations time to plan their offensives.

Afterwards, the Teutonic Order invaded Poland, annexing three strongholds: Dobrin, Bobrowniki, and Bydgoszcz. The contingent of Lithuanian light cavalry and Polish heavy cavalry met Teutonic Grand Master Ulrich von Jungingen's forces near the village of Grunwald (now in Poland). Ulrich von Jungingen army was also composed of Hungarian and Bohemian mercenaries, while Tartars and Bohemian mercenaries made up the Polish-Lithuanian ranks. Though the Lithuanian cavalry were the first to attack, they retreated first—the Teutonic Knights proved to be superior fighters. Leaving the Polish to fight alone, the Polish cavalry spent many hours attacking and defending but when they were exhausted and on the brink of defeat, the Lithuanian calvary regained formation and helped them to win.

To this day, the Battle of Grunwald is considered one of the most significant in medieval history, mostly because afterwards the Teutonic Order—who had been a major player in Europe—suffered much decline.

Decline

At the insistence of Jadwiga, who died childless in 1399, Jagiełło married Elizabeth Granowska, but she also died bearing him only a daughter. Two years later, he married a Lithuanian aristocrat, Sophia of Halshany. Two sons were born to his third wife, Władysław and Casimir.

When Władysław ascended the throne at a young age, it was already clear that there was dissent and opposition to the Lithuanian on the Polish throne. A conspiracy was planned to have Hedwig—Jagiełło's daughter to his second wife—married to Frederick of Brandenburg (Prussian aristocracy). Their conspiracy against the king fell through when Hedwig died (4). When Władysław was crowned king, Lithuania became recognized as a duchy or province within the Polish-Lithuanian Union. It still retained its sovereignty and could decide on internal and external matters in Eastern Europe.

A new force was rising in the East: the Ottoman Empire. Considered the Bulwark of Christianity, the Lithuanian-Polish forces envisioned victory against the Muslims with the aid of the Venetian Fleet. What the Lithuanian-Polish contingent did not see was that the Venetian Fleet actually transported the Muslims into Asia. In Varna (now Bulgaria), the Ottoman janissaries met the Lithuanian-Polish. Władysław died in battle, beheaded, with his head placed on a pike. The young king had not married nor had had any children.

Next in line was Casimir IV, Władysław's brother. Even before taking the throne, after the death of the Grand Lithuanian Duke Sigismund Kęstutaitis, Casimir was appointed as Grand Duke. There was so much outcry among the Polish nobles at Casimir becoming the Grand Duke that it also sparked conflict between the two countries. This is because Casimir had devoted much time to retracing his Lithuanian heritage, including learning the language and being baptized in Lithuania before being baptized in Poland. One of the most significant moves he made on being crowned King of Poland was to create a charter granting Lithuanian Boyars (members of the old aristocracy) much authority over their peasantry, giving them more political power and preventing the Polish kingdom from exercising complete rule over Lithuania.

The 16th century saw agricultural reforms introduced in the Grand Duchy helping Lithuania make incredible economic progress, which financed their wars with the Muscovites. Sadly, the power of Lithuania had been undermined to a large degree with their union with the Polish, causing Muscovy and Tartars to conquer lands including Novgorod, Tver, and Smolensk.

Conflict with Muscovy continued. From 1558 to 1583, Muscovy and Lithuania were embroiled in a tug-of-war for control over Livonia. Spanning three decades meant huge amounts of resources were needed to finance the war, forcing Lithuania to depend more on Polish assistance. Aid came, but at a huge price, namely the Union of Lublin. The terms of the Union stated decreed for the states to become one. Also, one third of the territory was annexed by the Polish. Though there was much discontent among Lithuanian nobility, the Grand Duchy after the three-decade war with Muscovy was in no position to fight back.

Despite being absorbed into the Polish kingdom, centuries later Lithuanians have still retained their unique identity, molded during the ascent of the Grand Duchy.

Certainly, the Grand Duchy was the most powerful state during the Geminid Dynasty. Its territory stretched from the Black to Baltic Sea. They were a driving force in the decline of the Teutonic Order. Finally, when they were in a subordinate position to the Polish, they continued to play to their advantages and endure. Centuries later, a distinct Lithuanian identity has been preserved.

CHAPTER TWELVE

THE KALMAR UNION

c. 1397–1523 CE

D espite the linguistic similarities and shared ethnic characteristics among the Nordic nations, they had failed to create a singular political entity. Nation-states such as England and Germany have numerous dialects—where some locals cannot understand others located in different parts of the country—yet a distinctly German or English identity has developed. We even saw, in the last chapter, the Lithuanians and Polish created a heterogeneous commonwealth that endured until the 17th century.

In fact, a union of Nordic nations called the Kalmar Union did take place. The Kalmar Union achieved considerable strength during the Late Middle Ages. However, unlike their German and British counterparts, it failed to conceive of a unitary nation-state or develop a stable, lasting empire. In this chapter, we will cover the quick rise and fall of the Kalmar Union.

Background

During the late 13th century, any alliance between the Danes, Norwegians, and Swedish seemed impossible. Between the Danes and

Swedish, there were two major conflicts: the War against Valdemar Birgersson (1274 to 1275) and the 6000-Mark War (1276 to 1278).

DENMARK AND SWEDEN

Valdemar Birgersson was elected king of Sweden in 1250, but truly became king in 1266 after Birger Jarl died. In 1274, he and his younger brother, Magnus Birgersson, went to war with each other. During the War, Magnus, their brother, Eric Birgersson, and King Erik V of Denmark allied to depose Valdemar Birgersson. As Valdemar's forces consisted principally of peasants whereas the alliance's were made up of Danish calvary (King Erik's calvary), the latter were victorious.

The Danish calvary hired by Magnus had come at a price, specifically 6000 marks. Erik signed an agreement naming the price, but Magnus refused to pay. Instead Magnus took the Danish by surprise and invaded their provinces, Halland and Skåne (in Sweden), in 1276. Magnus' tactics had worked—the Danish were defeated. A peace treaty was negotiated between the two nations; Magnus paid 4000 instead of 6000 marks in war reparations.

DENMARK AND NORWAY

Relations, if possible, were worse between the Danes and Norwegians. Legend has it that Danish noblemen conspired to kill their king Erik V, apparently stabbing him 56 times, and the Norwegians offered refuge to the murderers. Naturally, the Danish sought to avenge Erik V's regicide.

The conflict between the Danes and Norwegians had reached such heights that their king Erik VI partitioned parts of the land to be used as security bonds to pay for mercenaries in conflict against the Norwegians. As Denmark's efforts were mostly unsuccessful, German principalities claimed their newly acquired territories. By the time Christopher II took to the throne 1332, "the Danish realm ceased to exist" (Larrea, B.E., 2021).

Mini Ice Age and Great Famine

Conditions in Northern Europe got much worse at the turn of the 14th century. There were two main causes of this decline: the Mini Ice Age and the Black Plague. Though most of Europe was devastated by the Mini Ice Age and subsequent Great Famine (1315 to 1317), Northern Europe was the worst afflicted. Beñat Elortza Larrea, an associate professor who specializes in Medieval Scandinavian history, provides more insight.

> [T]his population crisis coincided with the opening stages of the Little Ice Age that affected Europe ... the chief effect of the rapid cooling was the Great Famine, which affected northern Europe between 1315 and 1322. The Danish Annals of Essenbæk aptly highlight the hardships that the famine brought with it: in addition to starvation, disease outbreaks and revolts became commonplace, as farming communities struggled to navigate the ravages of warfare, famine and unforgiving taxation (Larrea, B.E., 2021).

In 1349, a plague-infected ship arrived at the harbor of Bergen in west Norway. Soon the Black Death swept across the Nordic states decimating their populations. Historians explain that the Great Famine exacerbated the effects of the Black Death. When people are starving, they have much less resilience against disease. A third of the Swedish and Danish populations died. Norway, where the plague entered Scandinavia, was the worst affected, losing half their population.

Hanseatic League

A relic from Chapter 10 comes in the form of Henry the Lion, the cousin who abandoned Barbarossa. After doing so, he returned to expand the Duchy of Saxony. One key move he made was to found the city Lübeck. To this day, the city serves as a major port in Northern Germany, but it was thanks to Henry's negotiations and treaties with the

Swedish princes, merchants of Gotland, and Novgorod that produced the strength of Lübeck. In time, northern cities in Germany dominated the Danish straits and Baltic Sea.

We also saw in Chapter 10 that in the Holy Roman Empire, there was a move away from feudalism with the rise of the bourgeoisie. One class of people to emerge this time were traders and merchants. German traders prospered as the northern cities expanded their routes. It was at Lübeck where the eastern and western routes converged. As there was much interdependence between traders of both routes, a league was created to ensure German merchants maintained a monopoly of these waters. It was called the Hanseatic League.

Cities composing the Hanseatic League included Hamburg, Köln (now Cologne), and Lübeck. A clue to the significance of Lübeck in Germany's mercantile power then is in its full name Hansestadt Lübeck, meaning Hanseatic city of Lübeck. The term 'Hanseatic' derives from the German word Hansa meaning 'guild,' originating from an even earlier Gothic word meaning 'company' or 'troop.'

As mentioned, the chief motivation behind the League's formation was to monopolize the routes. The king had limited power and often allowed criminals off the hook for certain favors. Both the church and aristocracy were not especially interested in protecting merchants who threatened their power, so the traders had little choice but to band together. Whenever an extreme surge in trade and wealth occurs, criminality follows. In the case of sea routes: piracy.

> The overriding purpose of many of the associations that preceded the full league was to secure combined action against pirates and land robbers, and the need for such action always remained. With the same general intent, an increasing effort was also put into the provision of lighthouses, marker buoys, trained pilots, and other aids to safe navigation (Hibbert, A.B., 2022).

It soon became clear that the Hanseatic League was something to contend with. From 1368 to 1370, the Hanseatic League became embroiled in a war with the Kingdom of Denmark whose expansionist ambitions threatened their monopoly. One instance specifically was the Danish kingdom capture Øresund, a strait nested between Denmark and Sweden. Even today, Øresund is a commercial highway for maritime trade. The Hanseatic League attempted to regain power in Scandinavia by negotiating with the Swedish and Norwegians, but the Danish prevented such a move through diplomacy with the two Nordic nations. Soon it became apparent that Scandinavian unity was needed to stop the Hanseatic League.

Valdemar IV

Under Christopher II, the Danish lost plenty of their lands. Valdemar IV, his son, regained some of them. Being only 20 years old when he was proclaimed king, no one feared the young king much, so he was not asked to sign any charters. Except, Valdemar IV proved a shrewd and determined king. If he could not pay off the debt owed to the German merchants, he took it by war. Furthermore, marriage to the daughter of Eric II, Duke of Schleswig, gave him control over even more land, including parts of Jutland (land straddling Germany and Denmark) north of the Kongeå river.

It was against Valdemar IV that the Hanseatic League became involved in conflict, specifically over the island of Gotland in Sweden. Prior to these wars in the late 14th century, Valdemar took dramatic actions to ensure his heir ascended the Swedish throne. He captured Countess Elizabeth, forced her into a convent, and persuaded King Magnus to marry Valdemar's daughter, Margrete, to Magnus' son, Haakon VI of Sweden, in line for the throne. Magnus agreed to these nuptials, causing aristocratic families to rise up against him and force him to abdicate.

Albert of Mecklenburg believed he had greater claims to the throne. He was crowned king and ruled until 1389. It was not his death that ended his reign but rather his actions against the noble families. The king planned to introduce a reform that would reduce the size of their estates. Soon, his support in Stockholm was lost. It was with the impending reduction of their landholdings that the Swedish council turned to Margrete for help. At the Battle of Åsle, Margrete's troops met the king's. He was defeated and imprisoned. Rather than paying the hefty sum for retributions, Albert gave Stockholm up to Margrete. Though Margrete officially came to the throne in 1389, concluding Albert's 25-year reign, he still considered himself king until 1405 when he formally abdicated.

The Kalmar Union and Queen Margrete I

At six years old, Margrete was engaged to Haakon. At ten, she married him, and at 17, she went to Sweden to rule alongside him. At this age, she also gave birth to her first son, Olaf II. In 1375, her father, King Magnus, died. Margrete immediately secured Olaf's election as king of Denmark. Her sister, Ingeborg—possibly with greater claims— sought the same for her son, Albert, as his father—and her husband—was Duke Henry III of Mecklenburg. Nonetheless, Olaf was elected. As it stood, Margrete was married to Haakon, king of both Sweden and Norway, and her son was crowned King of Denmark, in line to succeed his father when she died. And Margrete ruled as Olaf's regent.

Before the events with Albert of Mecklenburg, Haakon died in 1380. Olaf succeeded him. Tragedy struck the royal family again; Olaf died in 1387 at age 17. As Queen Margrete had proven herself to be a capable ruler, in the next year, she was kept on as regent. One pivotal move Margrete had taken was during 1386 when she retook Duchy of Schleswig from German Holstein-Rendsburg counts. Not only was Schleswig significant territorially for both the Danish and Germans, but it proved politically useful for Margrete for she diminished the power of the Jutish nobles, who had previously had much influence before she secured the Duchy. With the gain of this Duchy, Margrete's role as regent was secure.

It was during this time that the Swedish asked for her assistance with Albert of Mecklenburg. After the victory at the Battle of Åsle, within a timeframe of three years, Margrete became the queen of all three countries.

Like most medieval royal families, securing the throne meant finding an heir as soon as possible. Though her role as ruler over Norway was guaranteed, if she did not assign a member of her kin as heir of all three thrones, claims could be made to Denmark and Sweden's thrones and the union of the kingdoms would collapse. In 1389, she announced her great-nephew, Eric of Pomerania, whom she adopted with his sister, to continue the dynasty. Since her nephew was only seven or eight years old then, she ruled as the regent once more.

THE CREATION OF THE KALMAR UNION

Though the three kingdoms were unified, Margrete wished to make this official. In 1397, Margrete invited the three *Riksråd* of the different countries to Kalmar (in Southern Sweden) to go ahead with this plan. A *Riksråd* was a council composed of nobility who co-ruled with monarchs. Naturally, Sweden, Norway, and Denmark had their own Riksråd. Elise Otte in the book *Scandinavian History* reveals that one of the principal motivations behind the Kalmar Union was the Hanseatic League.

> [T]he Queen said, that each one alone was a poor weak state, open to danger from every side, but that the three united would make a monarchy, strong enough to defy the attacks and schemes of the Hanse traders and all foes from the side of Germany, and would keep the Baltic clear of danger from foreigners (Otte, E., 1874).

Knowing that the councilors would not agree to establishing a single Nordic entity, Margrete assured them that their national identity was not under threat, nor would their laws change, and they would enjoy the same power as before. On June 17th, Eric of Pomerania was formally crowned king of the three nations; Queen Margrete would continue as his regent. The Kalmar Union was born.

EXPANSION, REFORM, NEGOTIATIONS, AND POLITICAL ALIENATION

Until her death in 1412, Margrete expanded the Kalmar Union. Under the policy of '*reduktion*' she regained all the property previously lost by

Denmark. One example was Gotland. The island's capital port, Visby, was of commercial significance. New territories were also acquired in the new world, like Vinland (in Canada). Finland too was acquired. A Swedish faction sought to use Finland as a base for expanding trade routes to the east with Russia, while the Danish intended for it to be used in trade routes to the south to prevent the monopoly of the Hanseatic League. Before she died, Queen Margrete tried to retake Schleswig by going to war with the Holstein. This war would continue under Eric's reign.

Like many notable rulers of the medieval period, Margrete soon realized the power of negotiations. Though the Kalmar Union was created to prevent the Hanseatic League from monopolizing the trade routes, one way the queen gained more power was actually by taking a step closer to the Germans. More Germans would be given officers in Denmark during this time. She also welcomed Danes and Swedes into high-ranking positions and formal offices, preferring to choose individuals for these roles who demonstrated great proficiency and skill. One of her main priorities was economic growth, as understandably the Nordic countries had been devastated by the Great Famine and Black Death. In Denmark she replaced the silver coins used as currency with the original copper tokens that had little value, bringing much wealth to the country.

A key contribution during her reign was helping to spread the Brigittine language. In 1344, a cloister of nuns was established by St. Bridget of Sweden. The saint not only had much influence on Catholicism but also the cultures of Germany and Sweden. Her dictations were recorded in Latin helping to evolve the Swedish language. During Margrete's reign, Brigittine language was encouraged throughout the Union, allowing Swedish terms and expressions to be borrowed by Danish and Norwegian.

Eric of Pomerania

The queen's nephew proved to be the best and worst of rulers. Eric's most notable policy was the Øresundtolden, introduced in 1429. The Øresundtolden was a toll ships had to pay to travel along Øresund. Not only was it immediately profitable, but this toll was maintained until 1857.

Sadly, Eric had instances where he managed the union poorly, ultimately leading to his and its downfall. Margrete preferred to deal with the Germans using negotiations; Eric of Pomerania preferred war. It is true that his great-aunt had started a war with the Holsteins before her death. It was this conflict that would plague the Kalmar until its dissolution. War was costly and the economic reform implemented by Margrete could not sustain the conflict.

Though the Holy Roman Empire declared that Southern Jutland belonged to the Kalmar Union, the Holsteins still invaded it. Andrew McKay's statement reveals Eric's lack of success in retaking Jutland: "When the war eventually ended, not only had there been no conquests but Eric controlled less of South Jutland than he had before the war started" (Mckay, A., 2019).

It was not only the Holsteins that Eric was at war with, but also the Hanseats. They both attacked Copenhagen. The king fled. In 1435, he signed an armistice with both, exempting them from the Øresundtolden, and he lost the Duchy of Schleswig to the Count of Holstein.

Engelbrekt Rebellion

Before signing the ceasefire, an anti-Danish rebellion broke out in Sweden the previous year. Due to the war with the Hanseatic and German counts, trade of Swedish iron was disrupted. Naturally, it was the miners who were the most impacted by the dropping value of iron. Tax was a heavy burden and Eric refused to negotiate with the Swedish *Riksråd*. That summer saw an uprising of miners and peasants who burned down the castle of Borganäs. A nobleman, Engelbrekt Engelbrektsson, led the rebellion, coining the name "Engelbrekt Rebellion." Eric and the rebellion attempted negotiations in August, but they fell through.

Though Engelbrektsson was assassinated in 1436, it was not before he met with the *Riksråd* and organized a march to Stockholm where Eric still had much loyalty and power. Erik Puke took over from Engelbrektsson but was executed in Stockholm in 1437. Though the Kalmar Union still existed, the Engelbrekt Rebellion encouraged Swedish claims for self-sovereignty.

Decline

Eric was deposed in 1397. His nephew, Christopher of Bavaria was elected as the next king. Since he was raised in Germany, Christopher had little experience with the Kalmar Union. As he too was elected by the Swedish and Norwegian *Riksråd*, it is clear that these councils held more power than him. Practically, this meant that the Kalmar Union no longer existed. Christopher became more of a puppet figure fulfilling the orders of these councilors. Soon after taking power, in 1441, peasant rebellions erupted in Jutland which Christopher brutally quashed, costing the lives of thousands. Subsequently, Christopher forbade peasants from brandishing weapons. With that law, the Danish peasants lost almost all freedom.

In 1448, he died. His eight-year rule ended and he left no heirs. Sweden elected Charles VIII as king. So did Norway the following year. The Counts of Holsteins chose Christian I. Following the Holsteins' lead, the Norwegians then elected Christian as their king, but the Swedish refused. From 1457 to 1467, Charles was deposed three times. After he died, Sten the Sture was elected as regent to the Swedish throne. In 1513, Christian II—grandson of Christian I—was elected as king and the Kalmar Union took its last breath.

Stockholm Bloodbath

Admittedly, it was a long final breath. The Swedish had resigned themselves to war with the Danes no matter what. So had Christian II. He proved to be a paranoid ruler who thought even his own loyalists would turn against him and claimed that his mistress was poisoned. In 1520, three days after he was crowned, he met the Swedish council who backed Sture. On August 8th and 9th, Christian and the nobles met an ecclesiastical court where he orchestrated to have them all executed. 82 were killed. Even those with a pro-Kalmar stance were murdered.

Gustav Vasa, whose father was one of the executed nobles in the Stockholm Bloodbath, made an alliance with Lübeck to avenge the murders. With the city's help, Sweden was regained under the Swedish council and the Kalmar Union ceased to exist.

War between Sweden and Denmark continued till the Napoleonic Wars. There would be 11 in total. After the Stockholm Bloodbath, the Kalmar Union ended. It was this massacre that put that final nail in the coffin, but it was the long-lasting wars with the Holsteins and Hanseats that truly eroded any union between the countries. Considering the conditions of the late 14th century and early 15th century, war was too costly. Trade and negotiation had proved superior; this was probably the reason why the Hanseats were able to defeat the Kalmar Union in 1435.

CONCLUSION

I t was the collapse of the Western Roman Empire that ushered in the Middle Ages. Ironically, it was the fall of the Eastern Roman Empire—Byzantium—that marked the end of this age. Though we did not cover Byzantium specifically, it remained as a peripheral figure, impacting every empire or kingdom that rose from the ashes of the former Western Roman Empire. After a siege spanning 53 days, the Ottoman army invaded Byzantium and the great three-walled city of Constantinople finally fell. The Middle Ages lost its enduring empire. And so, the Middle Ages began and ended with the loss of the two Roman Empires.

And honestly, what a period the Medieval Age was! The term Middle Ages, though it is stuck now in popular culture, hardly does this exciting age any justice. Dan Jones, a well-known and more accessible historian because of his television program touring British castles, offers the best summary of the Medieval Age. First, he says, "It is a repository of amazing stories" (Jones, D., 2021). Tales they have certainly been. While some of the headings may seem dramatic, like "The Scourge of God" or fanciful, such as "The Empire Strikes Back," that is exactly how they played out. Some of the most exciting stories were of espionage—and others perplexing, even humbling, like Attila the Hun turning back moments before the capture of Western Rome. Second, Jones also states that "Some of the greatest hits of history reside in this period" (Jones, D., 2021). These include the most grueling but also tactically brilliant battles, led by some of the sharpest generals like Charles Martel or William the Conqueror. This is generally where the Medieval period's bad reputation comes from—the countless brutal wars, as if any age is without them. We often forget the cultural contributions made by the Ottonian Renaissance or booming trade resulting in the creation of banking institutions, the adoption of Arabic-Indian numerals in place of the Roman ones, and the pinnacles of academic excellence, namely the building of Bologna University, Oxford University, and the University of Salamanca. There too was the introduction of new art forms: stained glass and tapestries. Even architecture, which we have hardly touched on, underwent a renaissance of its own with the Romanesque and Gothic styles. Finally—and probably the most underappreciated—were changes to agriculture, like the inventions of the heavy plough and horse collars, and innovating crop rotation, all aiding humans to produce more and more food so that our population could grow, withstand disease, and frankly, stop starving.

Medieval European Empires has tried to be an exciting read, providing you with the greatest hits of the medieval age: the prevalent empires, its leaders, famous battles, crucial inventions, a general understanding of what happened during the early, high, and late Middle Ages, and finally, insight of where much of present roots and history originate. Now you are armed with knowledge of this deeply fascinating age. Go out and share it with your family and friends. Test them. Teach them. And leave a comment if you found this read enthralling.

NOTES

Introduction

1. Ferrari derives from *ferraro* meaning 'blacksmith.' Think about the word 'Ferros'—the letters 'Fe' on the periodic table show the connection. It is the third most common surname in Italy—common like the British Smith.

2. The term Anglo-Saxon is used specifically to old Germanic peoples who came from Southern Scandinavia—therefore anyone from Angle or Saxon descent.

3. The Roman Empire was split into the Western Roman and Eastern Roman Empires. For the remainder of this book, the Eastern Roman Empire which survived from the 4th century to the 13th century will be referred to as Byzantium or the Byzantine Empire.

Chapter 1

1. While it may be an inane point to focus on, Istanbul is an intercontinental city—firmly positioned in Europe and Asia—qualifying the Byzantine capital, at least, as belonging to the European Empire. As the empire extended into the East, South, and Central parts of Greece, there is more evidence that

the Byzantine empire belonged to this continent.

2. The term Dark Ages initially referred to the whole of the medieval age. In more recent times it is has been restricted to just the Early Middle Ages. The length of the entire medieval age is about 1000 years, the quoted 700 years does not include the Late Middle Age that overlaps with the beginning of the Renaissance—durations are approximate, depending on when you choose the exact beginnings and endings.

Chapter 2

1. This is the Eastern Roman Empire with its capital at Constantinople. It will be referred to as Byzantium for consistency.

2. A Roman pound or 'libra' (from where we get the abbreviation lb) is estimated to be between 322 and 329 g—which differs from the modern definition of a pound, which is 456 grams (3 s.f.).

3. The Sassanid Empire is considered the last empire of the Persians.

4. The Walls of Constantinople are considered the last ancient fortification. The inner walls were 15 feet thick and 40 feet high.

5. Generalissimos had enormous influence in the empire because they commanded the army of the Empire. Some historians point out that the generalissimos having so much also contributed to the weakening state of the Roman Empire.

Chapter 3

1. The weather was colder than usual affecting the crop harvests leading to food shortages, as well as the increase of disease (Horgan, J., 2014).

2. The Justinian Plague, 540 to 549, ravaged Constantinople and killed 40% of its population. It spread to the rest of the Mediterranean, taking 25% of the population in the Eastern half.

3. An East Germanic tribe living in Eastern Europe who were defeated by the Lombards in 567.

Chapter 4

1. Jordan, Palestine, Israel, and Lebanon.

2. Outside of Medina and Mecca there were those who rejected Islam and who had converted as a result of the empire's expansion. Others were Islamic but opposed three members of the original *Rashidun.*

Chapter 7

1. From a linguistic perspective, the origins of the name 'Vikings' is interesting. Typically, one group of people name another group of people. For instance, the names 'Germany,' 'Britain,' and 'Africa' are all Latin derivatives. Another example is the word name of the country 'China.' We call the country 'China' but their own name is *'Zhōngguó'.* The Scandinavians came up with the words *'vik'* and *'Vikingr'* to differentiate the Vikings.

2. If the name Bluetooth sounds familiar it is not a coincidence. The short-range radio technology used in phones today, was named after this Viking as a nod to Scandinavia's contribution to telecommunications.

Chapter 8

1. Not at the time, but centuries later, these countries became their own nation states.

2. Specifically, the Royal Frankish Annals and Annals of Lobbes.

3. Alchemy is the ancient or medieval predecessor of chemistry.

4. Most likely it was a scribe writing on behalf of Charlemagne as it is believed the emperor could not read or write.

Chapter 9

1. Rollo the Walker was known as a formidable warrior. The reason he was given the nickname Rollo the Walker was because he was huge in physical stature thereby requiring no horse.

2. The Frankish fiefs were the Duchies of Normandy, Aquitaine, Burgundy, Brittany, and Gascony.

Chapter 10

1. Barbarossa was Frederick III (of Hohenstaufen), the son of Frederick II (of Hohenstaufen), but came to be known as Frederick I (of the Holy Roman Empire).

2. The Nazi's secret attack against the Russians during the Second World War was called Operation Barbarossa, paying homage to this German figure.

3. Apart from Rome, the city of Legnano is the only city named in the country's national anthem owing to this fateful battle.

4. Konrad von Hochstaden, the Archbishop of Cologne; Gerhard I von Dhaun, Archbishop of Mainz; Louis II, the Count Palatine; Ottakar II, King of Bohemia all voted for Richard while Albert I, Duke of Saxony; John I, Margrave of Brandenburg; Arnold II of Isenburg, Archbishop of Trier supported Alfonso.

Chapter 11

1. Though we are speaking about a mixed group of peoples, Ruthenians and Lithuanians, from now on we will refer to them as Lithuanians for easy comprehension.

2. There is some historical and nationalistic dispute about Olgerd or Algirdas' name. However, since Olgerd's own shield bore characters similar to Olgerd in Cyrillic, for more accuracy we will use Olgerd.

3. There is some mention among historians that owing to their affinity for paganism, the Lithuanians managed to establish somewhat friendlier relations with the Golden Horde.

4. There are some rumors that the Queen consort, Sophia, had poisoned her.

REFERENCES

- Adams, M. (2005) 'AUSTERLITZ THE BATTLE OF THE TWO EMPERORS', History today, 55(12), p. 30–. Available at: https://www.proquest.com/docview/202817945 (Accessed: 19 Jan 2023)

- Afsaruddin, A. (2019) 'Jizyah.' Encyclopedia Britannica. Available at: https://www.britannica.com/topic/jizya (Accessed: 11 Jan 2023)

- Astapenia, R. (2014) 'The History of the Great Duchy of Lithuania: Belarus'. Medieval Origins. Journal of Belarusian Studies 7, 2, 106-109, Available at: https://doi.org/10.30965/20526512-00702009

- Atkins, H. (2021). '10 of the Most Famous Vikings.' History Hit. Available at: https://www.historyhit.com/the-most-important-vikings/ (Accessed: 17 Jan 2023)

- Barbero, A. (2008) 'The Day of the Barbarians: The Battle That Led to the Fall of the Roman Empire.' Walker & Co.

- Baronas, D. (2006) 'The Encounter Between Forest Lithuanians and Steppe Tatars in the Time of Mindaugas'. Lithuanian Historical Studies 11, 1, 1-16, Available At: https://doi.org/10.30965/25386565-01101001

- Carson, T.E. (2002) 'Frederick I Barbarossa, Roman Emperor'.

New Catholic Encyclopedia. Available at: https://www.encyclopedia.com/religion/encyclopedias-almanacs-transcripts-and-maps/frederick-i-barbarossa-roman-emperor (Accessed: 19 Jan 2023)

- Cartwright, M. (2018) 'Feudalism.' World History. Available at: https://www.worldhistory.org/Feudalism/ (Accessed: 12 Jan 2023)

- Cartwright, M. (2020) 'Renaissance Humanism' World History. Available at: https://www.worldhistory.org/Renaissance_Humanism/ (Accessed: 21: Jan 2023)

- Červinskas, A. (2018) 'History of Lithuania.' Wutx. Available at: https://www.youtube.com/watch?v=EhoP-tqwVAw (Accessed: 20 Jan 2023)

- Choi, C.Q. (2016) 'The Real Reason for Viking Raids: Shortage of Eligible Women?' Live Science. Available at: https://www.livescience.com/56786-vikings-raided-to-find-love.html (Accessed 17 Jan 2023)

- Cohen, J. (2018) '10 Things You May Not Know About William the Conqueror.' History.com. Available at: https://www.history.com/news/10-things-you-may-not-know-about-william-the-conqueror (Accessed: 19 Jan 2023)

- Comyn, R. (1842) 'History Of The Western Empire, From Its Restoration By Charlemagne To The Accession Of Charles V'. London: W. H. Allen & co. and W. N. Wright

- Dash, M. (2012). 'Nice Things to Say About Attila the Hun.' Smithsonian Magazine. Available at: https://www.smithsonianmag.com/history/nice-things-to-say-about-attila-the-hun-87559701/ (Accessed 10 Jan 2023)

- de Jong, M. (2015) 'The Empire that was always Decaying.' Medieval Worlds comparative & interdisciplinary studies.

Available   at:
https://www.medievalworlds.net/0xc1aa5576%200x00329658.
pdf (Accessed: 18 Jan 2023)

- Duits, S. (2021) 'Holy Roman Empire'. World History. Available
  at: https://www.worldhistory.org/Holy_Roman_Empire/
  (Accessed: 19 Jan 2023)

- Fine, J.V.A. (1991) 'The early medieval Balkans a critical survey
  from the sixth to the late twelfth century.' 1st pbk. ed. Ann Arbor:
  University of Michigan Press.

- Fordham, M. (2017) 'The Norman Conquest 1065 -1087' Hodder
  Education.

- Gesparri, S. (2017) 'Venice and its neighbors from the 8th to 11th
  Century.' Leiden: Brill.

- Gibbon, E. (1777), 'The history of the decline and fall of
  the Roman Empire.', Dublin, 4th ed., vol. 1, Available at:
  https://link.gale.com/apps/doc/CW0103038221 (Accessed: 29
  Nov 2022).

- Gravett, C. (2003) 'Norman Stone Castles (1): The British Isles
  1066-1216'. Oxford: Osprey

- Halsey, E. (2020) 'The First Bulgarian Empire.' Study
  of Antiquity and the Middle Ages. Available at:
  https://www.youtube.com/watch?v=GYyjd3MtFIw (Accessed:
  16 Jan 2023)

- Hart, D. B. (2009) 'Atheist Delusions: The Christian Revolution
  and its Fashionable Enemies.' New Haven: Yale University Press.

- Heather, P. (1999) 'The Fall of the Roman Empire: A New History
  of Rome and the Barbarians.' London: Pan Books.

- Hibbert,   A.   B.   (2022).   'Hanseatic
  League.'   Encyclopedia   Britannica.   Available
  at: https://www.britannica.com/topic/Hanseatic-League

(Accessed: 21 Jan 2023)

- History.com Editors. (2018), 'Huns.' Available at: https://www.history.com/topics/ancient-china/huns (Accessed: 1 Dec 2022)

- History.com Editors. (2019) 'Vikings.' History.com. Available at: https://www.history.com/topics/exploration/vikings-history (Accessed: 17 Jan 2023)

- History.com Editors. (2020) 'Crusades'. History.com. Available at: https://www.history.com/topics/middle-ages/crusades (Accessed: 19 Jan 2023)

- Horgan, J. (2014) 'Justinian's Plague (541-542 CE)' World History. Available   at: https://www.worldhistory.org/article/782/justinians-plague-541-542-ce/ (Accessed: 24 Jan 2023)

- Jarnut, J. (1995). 'Storia dei Longobardi.' Milan: Einaudi. Italian edition.

- Jones, D. (2021) 'Is Genghis Khan harder than Jocko Willink?' Chris Williamson. Available at: https://www.youtube.com/watch?v=WNb7_e3Mi0I (Accessed: 24 Jan 2023)

- Jordanes, active 6th century (n.d.), 'The Origin and Deeds of the Goths.' Project Gutenberg. Available at: https://www.gutenberg.org/ebooks/14809 (Accessed: 1 Dec 2022)

- Karatay, O. (2003) 'In Search Of The Lost Tribe: The Origins and Making of the Croatian Nation' Çorum, Turkey: Karam Yayincilik

- Kennedy, H. (2022) 'The Prophet and the Age of the Caliphates: The Islamic Near East from the Sixth to the Eleventh Century (A History of the Near East)' 4th edn. Abingdon-on-Thames, UK: Routledge.

- Khan, S. M. (2020) 'Umayyad Dynasty.' World History Encyclopedia. Available at: https://www.worldhistory.org/Umayyad_Dynasty/ (Accessed: 11 Jan 2023)

- Knowledgia (2020) 'Why did The Lombards Collapse?' Available at: https://www.youtube.com/watch?v=71sjpwVaZ3A (Accessed: 4 Dec 2022).

- Kowalska-Pietrzak, A. (2015). 'History of Poland During the Middle Ages'. Available at: https://core.ac.uk/download/pdf/71989082.pdf (Accessed: 20 Jan 2023)

- Lane, F.C. (1963) 'Recent Studies on the Economic History of Venice', The Journal of economic history, 23(3), pp. 312–334. Available at: https://doi.org/10.1017/S0022050700104097

- Larrea, B. E. (2021) 'Medieval Scandinavia: war, plague, and the beginning of the Kalmar Union'. Medievalists. Available at: https://www.medievalists.net/2021/01/medieval-scandinavia-kalmar-union/ (Accessed: 21 Jan 2023)

- LDC (n.d.) 'World's Most Ancient Republic' Available at: https://www.ldchotels.com/en/magazin/worlds-most-ancient-republic/ (Accessed: 12 Jan 2023)

- Lucas, H.S. (1930), 'The Great European Famine of 1315, 1316, and 1317', Speculum, 5(4), pp. 343–377. Available at: https://doi.org/10.2307/2848143. (Accessed: 1 Dec 2022)

- Mark, J. J. (2014). 'Lombards.' World History. Available at: https://www.worldhistory.org/Lombards/ (Accessed: 2 Dec 2022)

- Mckay, A. (2019) 'Scandinavia's Kalmar Union.' Life In Norway. Available at: https://www.lifeinnorway.net/kalmar-union/ (Accessed 21 Jan 2023)

- Medievalists (2014) 'How the Saxons helped Charlemagne

become Emperor.' Medievalists. Available at: https://www.medievalists.net/2014/06/saxons-helped-charlem agne-become-emperor/ (Accessed: 18 Jan 2023)

- Melandsø, J. T. (n.d.), 'The Lombards in Italy – The History of a Kingdom. Learn about Italy.' Available at: https://learnaboutitaly.com/history/lombardy/687/lombards-ita ly-history-kingdom/ (Accessed: 2 Dec 2022)

- Modi, J. J. (1917), 'The Early History of the Huns.', Asiatic Papers, Part II. Bombay: The Times Press, pp. 293-349. Available at: https://fid4sa-repository.ub.uni-heidelberg.de/3333/1/Modi_Hi story%20of%20the%20Huns.pdf (Accessed: 1 Dec 2022)

- Norwich, J.J. (2012) 'History of Venice', 2012 edn. London: Penguin.

- O'Connor, B.B. (n.d.), 'The Dark Ages debate.' Available at: https://www.khanacademy.org/humanities/whp-origins/era-4-regional/43-a-dark-age-betaa/a/read-the-dark-ages-debate-be ta (Accessed: 28 Nov 2022)

- Otte, E. (1874) 'Scandinavian History.' New York: Macmillan Publishers.

- Paul the Deacon. (1974). 'History of the Lombards.' Philadelphia: University of Pennsylvania Press.

- Pruitt, S. (2016) '6 reasons the Dark Ages weren't so dark.', History.com. Available at: https://www.history.com/news/6-reasons-the-dark-ages-were nt-so-dark (Accessed: 10 Jan 2023)

- Pruitt, S. (2019) 'What was life like for Women in the Viking Age?' History.com. Available at: https://www.history.com/news/what-was-life-like-for-women-in-the-viking-age (Accessed: 17 Jan 2023)

- Rawlins, G.J.E. (2008) 'Rebooting Reality'. Available at: https://web.archive.org/web/20081223185836/http://www.roxie

.org/books/shoulders/ch02-labor.html

- Rowell, S.C. (2014) 'Lithuania Ascending: A Pagan Empire within East-Central Europe, 1295–1345'. Cambridge, UK: Cambridge University Press

- Searle, E. (1988) 'Predatory Kinship and the Creation of Norman Power, 840–1066'. Berkeley: University of California Press

- Story, J. (n.d.) 'The Viking Raid on Lindisfarne. English Heritage.' Available   at: https://www.english-heritage.org.uk/visit/places/lindisfarne-priory/History/viking-raid/ (Accessed: 17 Jan 2023)

- Szente-Dzsida, A. and Hollis, M. (2019) 'Huns: The Origin' Kings and Generals. Available at: https://www.youtube.com/watch?v=bFpQjWtpHcM (Accessed: 10 Jan 2023)

- Teodorani, A. (2019). 'Charlemagne: The Father of Europe'. Biographics. Available at: https://www.youtube.com/watch?v=J34_Qog2O8k (Accessed: 18 Jan 2023)

- The Editors of Britannica. (2012) 'Mayor of the palace.' Encyclopedia Britannica. Available at: https://www.britannica.com/topic/mayor-of-the-palace (Accessed: 18 Jan 2023)

- The Editors of Britannica. (2020) 'Rashidun.' Encyclopedia Britannica. https://www.britannica.com/topic/Rashidun (Accessed: 11 Jan 2023)

- The Editors of Britannica. (2020) 'Viking.' Encyclopedia Britannica. Available at: https://www.britannica.com/topic/Viking-people (Accessed: 17 Jan 2023)

- The Editors of Britannica. (2021) 'Middle Ages.' Available at: https://www.britannica.com/event/Middle-Ages (Accessed: 1

Dec 2022)

- The Editors of Britannica. (2022) 'Roman numeral.' Encyclopedia Britannica https://www.britannica.com/topic/Roman-numeral (Accessed: 12 Jan 2023)

- The Editors of Britannica. (2022). 'The Carolingian renaissance and its aftermath. Britannica.' Available at: https://www.britannica.com/topic/education/The-Carolingian-renaissance-and-its-aftermath (Accessed: 18 Jan 2023)

- The Saylor Foundation. (n.d.) 'The Umayyads: The First Muslim Dynasty.' Available at: https://resources.saylor.org/wwwresources/archived/site/wp-content/uploads/2012/07/HIST101-9.2-Umayyads-FINAL.pdf (Accessed: 11 Jan 2023)

- Treaty of Verdun. (2022). Oxford Reference. Available at: https://www.oxfordreference.com/view/10.1093/oi/authority.20110803115500937 (Accessed: 18 Jan 2023)

- Walsh D. (2013) 'Engineering the Viking Longboat' The American Society of Mechanical Engineers. Available at: https://www.asme.org/topics-resources/content/engineering-the-viking-longboat (Accessed: 17 Jan 2023)

- Whately, C. (2013) 'Jordanes, the Battle of the Catalaunian Plains, and Constantinople', Dialogues d'histoire ancienne, S 8(Supplement8), pp. 65–78. Available at: https://doi.org/10.3917/dha.hs80.0065.

- Wright, R. (1982) 'Late Latin and Early Romance in Spain and Carolingian France' Birkenhead, UK: Francis Cairns (Publications)

Acknowledgments

To Lauren whose incredible research, ability, and enthusiasm for the subject went into this book. To the KX10 team, especially Jana and Dane, who have provided constant support and advice throughout the project.

BOOKS PLANNED FOR THE FUTURE

Medieval Asian Empires

Medieval American Empires

Medieval African Empires

Made in the USA
Monee, IL
20 May 2023